Why Trial Attorneys Have Grey Hair

by Richard T. Sinrod, Esq.

DORRANCE
PUBLISHING CO
EST. 1920
PITTSBURGH, PENNSYLVANIA 15238

Dorrance Publishing Co
585 Alpha Drive
Suite 103
Pittsburgh, PA 15238
Visit our website at *www.dorrancebookstore.com*

ISBN: 978-1-6453-0268-1
eISBN: 978-1-6453-0868-3

Table of Contents

TO SEE THE LIGHT

How great it was, every day just right,
Living on top of the mountain, the light so bright,
People needing you to show them the way,
The smiles on their faces were all they had to say.
Each day I did battle like a soldier at war,
Trading thought and words, it helped me to soar,
The court is like a prizefighting ring, not all can enter,
The juries try hard, the truth they must render.
Then it all ended in the blink of an eye.
The bubble burst; they said surely I will die.
Doctors did as they promised and made the repair,
But they couldn't help leaving me desperate and in despair.
It hasn't been easy, that truth I must share.
Were it not for a special woman, I wouldn't be here.
She simply doesn't know the meaning of quit.
Oh, what a warrior, the epitome of grit.
I've tried many things to get out of my rut.
"Stand up, husband," she says, and show me some gut,
Climb out of your darkness and come see the light,
Open your eyes and see all that is right.
And so, taking the lead of many a sage,
I've gone back in history by turning back the page,
Remembering for how long legal wars I did fight,
I'm hoping to look back and by doing so again see the light.
Sometimes it's hard to see what's true,
So much has happened to darken my view.
But I keep on writing and those smiles I see make me feel proud.
I can see forward, like magic, light through a cloud.

Dedicated to my wife, Yael, for whom the bell tolls

Preface

Having entered college before my seventeenth birthday, I became an attorney at the ripe old age of twenty-three. To describe me as nervous during my first court appearances would be an understatement. I quickly learned that trial work was more than a full-time job; it required an absolute commitment to the client and the law, and a flair for the courtroom arena. As time went by, I worked on creating a unique style and approach to my profession, whether it was in high-stakes personal injury law or in challenging criminal cases. At first, it seemed like trying to reinvent the wheel. However, I was fortunate to find myself doing battle with incredibly skilled attorneys. Slowly, I learned from them and tried to adopt the best traits of each adversary. It might be a gesture, a mannerism, a way of phrasing questions, or a knack for using an analogy to make a point—together they all helped me polish my skills.

One of the pleasures of the law for me was the camaraderie among members of the profession. There is a mutual respect that enables the best trial attorneys to lock horns, make the best presentation they can on behalf of their client, and then, when the case is over, shake hands and join their adversaries for a drink and perhaps dinner. I compare it to watching two hockey teams competing fiercely in the Stanley Cup Finals and then, true to tradition, lining up and shaking hands, sometimes hugging their opponents, out of genuine respect. The biggest thrill, though, is the realization that your hard work has resulted in a fundamental improvement to the life and well-being of your clients, who have placed their future in your hands.

For nearly forty years, I relished my role as a trial attorney, but all that came to a sudden end when a dissecting aortic aneurysm—a tear in the main artery leading to the heart—nearly took my life and left me with cognitive impairments that forced me into early retirement. Whereas I was once able to deliver an hourlong summation without a single note, I found myself struggling with short-term memory loss. I spent several years like a ship in the middle of the sea without a rudder. It was truly the love and strength of character of my wife, Yael, that kept me from drowning. Finally, about fifteen years ago, I decided that I owed it to her and my children to do something positive with the remainder of my life. I needed something to replace the thrill that courtroom jousting had provided. My first project was to become a coach for the Mock Trial Program at a local high school in Dutchess County, New York, where we then lived. After four years, our success rate made me realize that I could use my legal skills to further benefit the public. Confident that some of my students would go on to successful careers in the legal profession, I then decided to write these chapters in the hope that the public would find these cases as fascinating as I did and benefit from my experience. Fortunately, my long-term memory was intact, so I could recall the cases in vivid detail. Each chapter was a cathartic experience. As I composed each story, I took pride in remembering how good a trial attorney I was, but at the end of each chapter, the realization of what I could no longer do was depressing. That is why it took me so many years to finish this book; I needed time between chapters, knowing the path that lay ahead.

It was a challenging journey, but now that I have set these stories down, I hope readers will find them enlightening and instructive. They should be of particular interest to those who may be entering the field of law or called to serve on a jury in these turbulent times. What better example is there of the premise that we all must live in harmony than the fundamentals of our jury system, which I believe to be the best in the world. Twelve people from all walks of life, strangers, come together to sit as impartial jurors. Sworn to hear the case fairly by placing their hand upon the Bible, they are reminded by the judge that they should listen to each other, respect each other's thoughts, and come to a uniform decision true to their oath. Would not the world be a better place if we all functioned in that manner, with mutual respect for each other? I leave you to be the judge.

Assault With a Deadly Weapon

Having been a part of the ad hoc law firm that initiated the famous Agent Orange litigation, I am proud to say that I assisted in bringing about a major change in how the statute of limitations is to be applied. Every claim for monetary damages must be brought within a statutory time limit, known as a statute of limitations, and there is often an issue as to when the statute begins to run. Until the Agent Orange decision, the plaintiffs would have been timed-barred from commencing their claims, since their exposure to this dioxin-laden chemical took place years before, in their service in Vietnam. However, since the toxic effect was not discovered until years after their exposure and affected not only them but also their unborn children, applying the normal limitation statute in the normal way would have resulted in a gross injustice. New York State met this dilemma head-on and carved out a new statutory scheme by starting the running of the time limitation from the date of discovery, or when discovery should have been made, and if the years gone by already had run their course, an additional window of one extra year was created to correct the inequity.

The case I am about to present has nothing to do with the Agent Orange litigation, but it illustrates my application of that legal decision's logic to a plaintiff who was about to lose his case if my analogy proved to be unsuccessful.

Lance[1] was a young, gay man in his mid-twenties. While he chose to keep his own apartment, paid for by his lover, most of his time was spent with his lover at the lover's apartment—a fancy, custom-decorated place located in a luxury building in an upscale part of town. That lover was an attorney who was a partner in a major law firm. I am unsure whether anyone at the law firm

---

[1] Names and identifying details of many individuals mentioned in this book have been changed to protect their privacy.

I

was aware of this relationship. While homosexuality had already entered the mainstream of society, its ramifications were the talk of the day because the association between homosexual behavior and the AIDS epidemic had been confirmed. Still, discovery would have most likely meant an immediate loss of his lover's equity partnership in the firm.

In keeping with the times, Lance's partner carried the secret of his AIDS affliction to his early death. Lance came for legal help following that death, after going through personal papers of his now-deceased significant other and discovering that for almost three years, the deceased had clearly known that he was HIV-positive and was under treatment. Seeing this, Lance had himself screened and discovered that he had an abnormal T-cell count, a pathway to a full-blown HIV-positive diagnosis. The records also indicated that the partner was not exactly faithful in claiming a monogamous relationship with Lance. After examining all of the facts, we brought an initial application to examine the deceased's medical records, which until that time were confidential, even after death. Taking advantage of certain health department rules concerning the requirement that a physician report such cases when discovered, we were able to persuade a court to conduct an *in camera* inspection of the medical records and turn over anything relevant to our claim to us. The records turned over to us made it clear that we had a good case against the estate of the deceased, based upon a theory that the deceased had purposefully and knowingly had unprotected sex with our client while the deceased was aware that he was HIV-positive and dying of AIDS. The problem we faced was that more than three years had gone by since the deceased's passing, so that if we claimed the act to be intentional or negligent, the applicable statute of limitations had run out. The only chance we had was to convince a court that the HIV infection was the equivalent to exposing our client to a deadly, noxious substance, like dioxin, the deadly component in Agent Orange.

Following that logic, the statute of limitations should not begin to run until the date of discovery, or whenever it should have been discovered, adding an additional one-year window if the normal statute had already run out.

"Fat chance," said my scholarly friends. War heroes are one thing, but "these people, that's something else," they suggested. "Well, you never know if you don't try" was my answer to the skeptics. Action commenced, followed by an immediate motion to dismiss the case after claiming that the statute of limitations had run out. The motion was granted and the case was dismissed, as expected. An immediate appeal was filed and after the usual calendar wait of almost a year, oral argument was finally heard in the appellate court. By this time, the case had engendered much publicity since it had far-ranging implications. Although I had started my career doing appeal work, it had been at least twenty years since I had appeared in an appellate court. The case was called near the end of the court calendar, so I had the benefit of listening to many arguments, trying to size up each of the seven judges, particularly how to answer their questions and which of them were more actively involved than the others.

Although it was risky, I tried for a little levity right from the beginning. I explained to them that it had been about twenty years since I had last been there and added, "I'm amazed, in those twenty years, how astute and learned in the law you have all become." When one quickly quipped, "It's obvious that your powers of observation must have improved over those years," they all started to laugh, and I knew I had gained their attention, if not their respect. The nerves now gone, I must say that my presentation was spot-on, so when I left the courtroom, I felt sure of victory. My instincts proved correct when three weeks later, the court reversed the lower-court decision dismissing the case, reinstated the action, and directed that the case move forward with all deliberate speed. Even before the defendant estate's answer was received, telephone conferences started, during which I learned that more than $250,000 in legal fees had already been incurred by the estate. The executor finally came to the realization that settling was a far better decision than continuing to dole out unconscionable sums of money in defending the case, thereby exhausting all estate assets. We agreed to split the estate: one half went to my client, and the other half remained in the estate.

How many other inflicted plaintiffs may have benefited from this decision, I will never know. I do know that I lived up to my obligation and that of my profession that everyone is entitled to an attorney. And when looking in the mirror, it's great to know that the guy looking back improved the lives of many whom he will never know.

Can Money Buy You Happiness?

These days, when you turn on the television, you are bombarded with commercials by pharmaceutical manufacturers informing you about their latest miracle drug. After a pitch for the claimed benefits of their product, usually by paid performers in a panoramic setting, next comes the mandatory list of side effects, ranging from a rash to agonizing death, all of which make you wonder why anyone would take the drug to begin with. Maybe that's why they are called "miracle drugs," since it is a miracle that anyone would be stupid enough to take the drug and put their life at risk. "Ask your doctor," the actor says. The advertisers forget to tell you that the doctors have been lobbied, supplied with a free batch of their potion, and offered a free trip to a paradise island of their choice if they prescribe enough of their wares. In years gone by, it was a traveling minstrel show; now it's your TV.

Ralph was the victim of one of these flimflams. He was a longtime sufferer of painful arthritis in his lower back. When the latest miracle drug came along, promising him relief from his chronic pain, Ralph took notice. After seeing a commercial, he ran to his doctor and asked him to prescribe the drug. This was long before the requirements of today that warnings of side effects be clear and concise.

So, his doctor, knowing Ralph was truly in chronic pain, prescribed the drug, and Ralph's pain eased, much to everyone's delight. Ralph's enjoyment of life improved to the point that he and his wife were able to go on a vacation for the first time in years and they could resume dancing with each other, an activity that brought them joy as if they were teenagers. These improvements had the effect of blinding them to the gradual urinary problems that Ralph began to experience after taking the drug for about a year. He returned to the doctor, who sent Ralph to a urologist for a diagnosis. After evaluating and examining Ralph, the urologist studied the history, investigated, read the latest literature, and began to suspect the miracle arthritis drug was the cause of the problem. He eventually discontinued its use and prescribed another, more standard, arthritis medication. Lo and behold, the truth began to emerge that the manufacturer had not been candid about side effects that it knew about during development of the drug but failed to disclose.

The lawsuit that I initiated on behalf of Ralph and his wife, Alice, was one of the first to be brought against the company over this medication, followed not long thereafter by a class-action suit on behalf of all victims who had developed kidney damage after taking the drug for extended periods of time. Not wanting to prejudice its position in the class-action suit, the manufacturer approached me and made an offer we could not refuse, conditioned upon confidentiality—a practice that I believe should be prohibited to protect the public by denying manufacturers the ability to hide the danger of their product from the public. Ralph was happy with the outcome, and his kidney damage apparently was not permanent or disabling, so it was a seemingly joyous Ralph and Alice who agreed to the settlement, signed the release papers, and came into my office to receive their share of the settlement recovery.

I always made it a practice to personally hand the money to my client, affording me the opportunity to share in their joy and remind them to remember me in the future and refer anyone they knew who needed the services of their brilliant attorney. I must admit that I was concerned when they asked me whether they could get a portion of their share in cash. This was not the first time that such a request had been made. I would usually call my bank to tell it to expect one of my clients and that it was OK to allow them to cash the check. In this case, however, it was the amount of money they wanted in cash that caused my concern. It was not the usual $500, or $1,000, or even $3,000 a client had asked for. The news that they wanted to cash a check for $30,000 shocked me. They lived in a downtrodden section of town, so I expressed concern about their safety and the chance that they might be robbed. Although I was reluctant to probe deeply, I nevertheless asked a number of questions, hoping to get the reason for their request. "Do you owe a bookie, a shylock, someone dangerous?" I asked, among other questions. After each query, they looked at each other and refused to answer. I finally gave up, called the bank, wrote out two checks—one for $30,000 to cash immediately and the other for the balance of their share—and sent them to the bank. When the bank called to make sure they were my clients, I spoke to Ralph and asked him to call me when they got home so I could rest easy that they had arrived safely, which they did.

It was about three weeks later that I heard from Ralph, who explained that he and Alice were in the area and wanted to come in to say hello. Of course, I said yes, and I greeted them warmly after they hugged me and thanked me for all I had done for them. There was something about their demeanor that made me curious. Ralph and his wife were both no more than five feet, seven inches tall. Both could best be described as portly and stood absolutely no chance of ever appearing in a racy calendar. There was something, though, that made them appear different that day—a spring in their step maybe, something I could not understand. I finally asked again, "Why the need for the $30,000?" It was then that they finally agreed to tell me the story. It seemed that they both had the same fantasy. To fulfill that fantasy, they went to the bank, cashed the $30,000 check in $100 bills, and went home to act it out. They spread the money out all over their bed and proceeded to have what they described as the most exhilarating, wild, satisfying sex they had ever experienced. I must admit that this scenario has never been something that I would consider sexually arousing. I do, however, laugh when I think about the old cliché that money cannot buy you happiness. If you believe that, let Ralph and Alice's story prove that money can bring you happiness, if only for a fleeting moment of ecstasy!

Conscious Pain and Suffering

Part of the health care reform debate that has raged in recent years is the issue of tort reform, which is touched upon in one of my later chapters. With all of the many issues this debate includes, I cannot help but wonder why many of those opposing health care reform list tort reform, including the contentious issue of frivolous medical malpractice lawsuits, as their number one issue. As of early 2020, jury verdict reports indicate that 67 percent of these cases were resulting in verdicts in favor of the defendants, while less than 1 percent of the premium dollar was being paid out to settle claims and/or pay judgments awarded by either juries or after appeals from jury awards. On top of that, death rates as a result of hospital malpractice continue to rise, even in states that have enacted tort reform, including caps on pain and suffering awards, undercutting the case for reform.

During jury selection, prospective jurors often express concern about large awards in malpractice cases. The reason can be anything from using this issue to argue that they can't be impartial, in order to be excused, to a true belief in what they say, often a result of the constant barrage of misinformation put out by lobbyists for the insurance companies. To sincere prospective jurors, a series of questions pointing out that the jurors making those awards were people like them who, by hearing all the evidence, are in the best position to know what fair and reasonable compensation was in that case, will often persuade them that they can put aside their concerns and sit in judgment in the case before them. Those who truly understand our jury system uniformly agree that while it is imperfect, it is the best in the world. To those who disagree, ask yourself whether tort reform would have had a negative impact upon the impartial jurors' judgment of the case of Kelly Smith.

In was in the early 1970s that Kelly entered the hospital to give birth to her third child. At the time of their marriage, Kelly and her husband had decided that they wanted four children. A boy and a girl, ages five and three, already enjoyed life in this close, happy, and joyous family. Knowing their parents' intentions, the children eagerly awaited the new baby and the opportunity to help. For the past three months, the new baby seemed to be the focus of attention in all discussions. Age-appropriate discussion had taken place to help the children understand that instead of the natural childbirth that brought them into the world, the new baby would be delivered by a C-section. So, when Kelly went into labor, hugs and kisses were exchanged, and off everyone went to bring mom to the hospital on this joyous occasion. Mom was left at the hospital after more kisses and some tears, and the family went home to await the news. The new brother was born the next day, but that was not the only news. The children were told that there would be a delay in their mom coming come. How long a delay was uncertain. The baby was fine and would be home on schedule, which took the edge off their concern about mom. The children's tender age prevented their dad from offering a full explanation of why his heart was so heavy.

It seems that during the surgical procedure and while mom was being intubated by the anesthesiologist, something had gone terribly wrong. An improper insertion of the intubation tube caused Kelly to regurgitate into the tube, and the stomach liquid was allowed to enter her lungs, resulting in severe damage to the interior of the lungs. This prevented her from breathing normally, causing her to fall into a coma. It also resulted in brain damage due to ischemia, or lack of oxygen to the brain. Kelly was in an unstable, life-threatening condition. She remained in that condition for thirty-four days, during which she required round-the-clock care, until, at the age of thirty, Kelly Smith was pronounced dead. Two children, one baby of thirty-four days, and her husband found themselves without their beloved mother and wife. The baby would never know his mother and would go through life knowing that she died bringing him into this world—a difficult burden for some to bear. The pain never left, weighing heavily on everyone.

A malpractice action was brought against the hospital and all medical professionals present in the operating room. In such an instance, two separate and distinct claims are made. One is for the pain and suffering caused to Kelly, and the other is for her wrongful death, on behalf of those who suffered economic loss by reason of her death. Although Kelly was not employed and therefore there was no future loss of income, the law recognizes that the services performed by a mother and wife can be quantified and an expert economist is permitted to testify and offer evidence and an opinion as to the value of these services, measured until the children reach adulthood. The pain and suffering claim, in this case, can be for only thirty-four days. Fear of dying had, by that time, been recognized by the law as an element of damage. An example is a passenger in a plane that encounters trouble at forty thousand feet. The pilot fights to keep the plane aloft for ten minutes after announcing the peril, and then the plane crashes and all aboard are killed. The hurdle that the plaintiff's attorney must overcome, however, is that the plaintiff must be CONSCIOUS AND AWARE of his or her pain and suffering to be entitled to an award for conscious pain and suffering. What about Kelly, who was in a comatose state for those thirty-four days? While it was agonizing for all her family members who were allowed to stand vigil in her room, how does the attorney submit objective proof of her pain and suffering and her fear of death?

There are several levels of coma, starting at Level I, the mildest degree, up to Level VIII, the deepest degree of coma. This is the scale formulated on the West Coast and known as the Rancho Los Amigos Levels of Cognitive Functioning. After years of study, physicians have learned that, depending on the coma level, a patient in a coma, no matter how prolonged, can actually hear the sound of the spoken word, retain the spoken words, and relate them if the patient recovers from the coma, regaining consciousness. Patients may also sense and describe physical pain and emotional issues experienced during the coma, again depending on the level of coma. It is one thing, however, if the patient comes out of the coma and another if they never do.

Yes, a loved one can describe events that suggest awareness on the part of the patient, but will they be believed in the face of medical records to the contrary? That is why the best evidence, critical evidence, can sometimes be found in a portion of the medical record labeled nurse notes. Nurses are required to document all they see and do while in the presence of the patient. Since a doctor's note can sometimes be seen as self-defensive, nurses can often be deemed more objective, depending on circumstances.

Nurses have often been described as guardian angels. Nothing could be truer than in the case of one of Kelly's nurses who may have spent as much or more time at her bedside than any other nurse. On the twenty-sixth day, the following entry appeared in her notes: "I was at her [Kelly's] side and, while adjusting the pillow, I said, 'How are you doing today?' Her eyes moved in my direction and she appeared to respond to me by blinking. When I said, 'Can you hear me?', she blinked again, and a tear came into her eyes." Based on this entry, our firm decided to gamble and go ahead with the case, which included calling in the foremost expert in anesthesiology, at a cost of $5,000 for the consultation, with no guarantee of his opinion, and $10,000 for his courtroom appearance at trial. Please keep in mind that if you lose, since the fee is contingent upon recovery of damages, there is no fee, and often the client does not have the money to reimburse you for the expenses you have advanced. With a lump in my throat, I took the chance that his testimony would be worth every penny, and our judgment proved to be correct when the judge agreed that the nurse's notes were admissible in evidence and that the jury could conclude that Kelly was aware of her surroundings during her comatose state, if they chose to do so. They must have, because after three hours of deliberation, the jury awarded $450,000 for the wrongful death of Kelly and $2,550,000 for her conscious pain and suffering and fear of dying.

To those who advocate tort reform, I ask you to place yourself on that jury, the jury that knows more about this case than you will ever know, and then ask yourself whether justice will be served by awarding the Kelly family a fraction of the amount that this jury found to be fair and reasonable. If your answer remains that you are in favor of tort reform, please remember to express this opinion if you are ever summoned to jury duty. I can promise that you will be excused from ever sitting on a jury, which most believe, after serving as a juror, to be the most important civic duty of their life.

Cross-Checked

Marriage is a wonderful institution, although, with about 35 to 40 percent of marriages ending in divorce, I suppose a strong argument could be made to the contrary.

The only thing I am sure of is that if I were still practicing law, I would avoid any matrimonial cases. I practiced law for thirty-five years as a trial practitioner and studiously avoided all but three requests that I represent one of the parties in a matrimonial action. Sometimes a past client will not take no for an answer.

In the mid-1970s, matrimonial law went through a metamorphosis, referred to as equitable distribution, resulting in a significant number of attorneys taking up matrimonial law. This caused divorce cases to become an accounting exercise, with fault literally becoming irrelevant. Some of the attorneys who became divorce lawyers truly became leaders in their new field. Others should have gone on to alternate areas of law.

Divorce attorneys are best served by turning off their phone at nights. As with physicians, clients seem to think that you are on duty twenty-four hours a day and that regardless of the hour, you are sitting there waiting to deal with their petty problems, which can be anything from a visitation issue to "my husband refuses to put the toilet seat down, no matter how many times I complain."

After the first "no" was ignored, I usually went on to tell the prospective client that, no matter what, the children come first. Usually, that admonition was enough. If not, my request for a LARGE retainer did the trick.

Well, if it weren't obvious by now, when Bill Johnson called, he wouldn't take no for an answer, no matter what I tried to use as an excuse. I must admit that his yearly business retainer caused me to melt like ice on a sunny day. Perhaps it was only my wife of fifty-two years who for the first time taught me how to react to the word no!

Little did I know that the marriage between Bill and Beth, which lasted about nine years, would be dwarfed by the length of their divorce battle and post-divorce disputes, which lasted about fourteen years.

All went well during the first five years of their marriage, during which they had two children. It was when they felt that Bill was not being paid enough by his family-owned company that things started to unravel. A classic scheme was put into place whereby a dummy corporation was set up to act as a supplier. Checking accounts were created; P.O. boxes established; stationery, including invoices and receipts, printed; and before you knew it, Bill's company paid out hundreds of thousands of dollars for goods it never received.

Just who was involved in developing the scheme was never agreed upon by the parties. Bill said both of them. Beth said it was Bill alone. After investigation, including checking the handwriting on documents, I was convinced that Beth was involved from the very beginning. Fancy cars and a boat followed, with expensive jewelry and worldwide vacations thrown into the mix. The money also gave Bill the wherewithal to afford a fancy girlfriend.

The strain on both began to eat away at the core of their bond, and before long, Beth wanted a divorce. When Bill heard that, he apparently had an awakening, especially after talking to me, and he advised Beth that while she could have the divorce, he was going to tell the company about the dummy corporation scheme and attempt, however possible, to pay the money back. Beth's response was simple and to the point: if you implicate me, you will never see your children again! Bill was, of course, immediately fired from the family company.

Money issues were further complicated by the fact that no state or federal income tax had been paid, nor had any of the pilfered money been reported as income, which it was under both the IRS and state tax codes. When Bill advised Beth that he intended to follow my advice and file amended state and federal tax returns, she refused to cooperate and told Bill that he was on his own.

And so, the battle started, with issues of visitation, maintenance, and child support right there on the front burner to resolve. We were assigned to a judge to deal with all pretrial issues. About three weeks later, the soundness of my heart was put to the test when I walked into the courtroom of that judge on an entirely different matter, only to have him recognize me and say, in a tone that I cannot accurately describe, "Counselor, it's good you're here. Your client, Mr. Johnson, CALLED ME AT HOME LAST NIGHT, and you and I have something to discuss."

The best way to describe my feelings at the moment is extreme nausea, as usually the discussion the justice wanted to have was the costs, sanctions, and fine he intended to impose. While we walked into his private chambers, I felt into my pocket to see how much bail money I had. Imagine my shock when the judge proceeded to tell me that, as a churchgoing man with seven children, he was disgusted by the lack of concern fathers tended to show about their children during divorce proceedings and that he was pleased at the concern my client was showing about his children, particularly the summer camp he wanted to send them to, despite his present financial problems and the demands his wife was making upon him.

Of course, the conversation could not continue further without Beth's attorney present, so the judge scheduled a conference to address that, as well as related issues.

The only thought I had as I left his chambers was that I had just dodged the proverbial bullet.

I had never met Beth's attorney before this case, which was not surprising since he was an attorney who did a considerable amount of matrimonial work. Simon was a friendly enough fellow, and I actually took a liking to him.

Several weeks later, I happened to run into him in the courthouse cafeteria, which is how we came to be having a cup of coffee that day. We discussed the case in general terms, each trying to learn as much as we could from the other about their positions in the case and, as the saying goes, each trying to get into the other's head.

As I started to get up to leave, entirely out of my sometimes-wicked sense of humor, I said to Simon, "I want you to know—and Simon, I mean this from my heart—no matter what happens while this case is pending, I will never allow your relationship with Beth to become an issue." Two days later I received a

Notice of Change of Attorney from Simon, who went on to marry Beth one week after the divorce was final. Too bad I'm not that good at picking winners at the racetrack!

The next major battle arose several months later, when I received an urgent request to meet with Bill. In order to put the subject of that meeting into perspective, you must know that during the years leading up to the divorce proceeding and while it was pending, the home professional hockey team had won several straight Stanley Cup championships and was the hottest sports season ticket on the market. Bill, who had two season tickets, had just learned that when Beth received the subscription to the playoff tickets at the marital residence, which she had sole possession of, she went to the team headquarters, exercised the right of redemption, paid for the playoff tickets, and took them into her possession. No, it wasn't the crown jewels, but to Bill, all-out war had been declared. Offered a king's ransom for their return, I commenced a proceeding known as an Order to Show Cause to secure immediate return of the tickets and a stay preventing Beth from ever claiming the right to ownership of the subscription or from selling them. This application for an order is made on written papers known as an Order to Show Cause with Temporary Restraining Order, which shortens the time that must be given an adversary to respond to the application and also shortens the time for the matter to come before the judge to whom oral argument is made. The reason given is to prevent irreparable harm from occurring in the interim; in this case, games one and two of the Stanley Cup Finals would have been played before an application could be made by regular motion.

The proposed Order to Show Cause and supporting proof is brought to court and submitted to a judge randomly assigned to review the papers, but first a law clerk must review them to make sure that they are properly drawn. When the clerk saw the papers, his first reaction was to sneer and say, "No way." I finally convinced him that despite his priorities, beauty is in the eyes of the beholder. Imagine his surprise when he brought the papers back from the judge, signed, and setting the hearing for two days later. I believe his exact words were, "Boy, are you lucky that the judge is a hockey fan."

When I arrived in court with Bill for the oral argument, I believe it was a Friday. Bill and I met in the parking lot of the court. Procedurally, it was necessary for us to convince the court that it should direct that the Temporary Restraining Order become permanent; that Beth be directed to turn over the tickets to Bill, and that the hockey team be directed to send any future tickets to Bill at his address. Our evidence was solid, and we were confident of victory as we walked toward the court, almost oblivious to the many trucks parked near the building. It was not unusual to have media trucks in the area as sometimes a high-profile trial attracted their attention. Shock is an understatement when it turned out that OUR case was the attention-getter. There was a rush of reporters when someone identified me as the attorney on the case; the video and still cameras started, microphones seemed to come out of nowhere, and the interviews started. The case was already being discussed throughout the country. After the din subsided and the cameras were turned off, I asked one of the reporters if they didn't have anything else to do, and I was assured that this was the big story of the day.

The large courtroom was standing room only during the oral argument. Unexpectedly, the court issued its order right from the bench, in our favor. The rush to interview Bill on the way out was even more intense than the earlier frenzy, and during the day I received several telephone calls from throughout the country, not only seeking interviews but wanting us to appear on television. Beth and her new attorney, John Connors, seemed to disappear into the woodwork.

Pretrial discovery was long and arduous as issues of money and what constituted their standard of living were battled out. Cutting to the chase, the most cantankerous issue was whether the stolen money, a good deal of which was paid back by Bill by the time the case came up for trial, was to be included when computing what assets constituted the pot referred to as the marital assets and what income was to be included in computing Bill's ability to pay child support and maintenance. Beth continued to deny any involvement in the embezzlement, which promised to make the trial long and tedious.

As luck would have it, due to a heavy caseload, we were assigned to a criminal court judge who had never presided over a matrimonial trial in his eighteen years on the bench. I had never appeared before him, though my adversary had appeared before him on occasion, since he also practiced criminal law.

We came before the judge for a pretrial conference and discussed the many issues that were anticipated. Trying his best to forge a settlement, the judge made a recommendation regarding child support and visitation which, as far as I was concerned, was tantamount to including all the pilfered funds in the marital assets, demonstrating his lack of experience in matrimonial law and his desire to avoid having the case go to trial. My client and I refused, and I remember his words to this day. "OK, let's start, but just remember, Counselor, when putting in your proof, dribble near the basket and no outside shots, as you know what my ruling will be on the money issue." Not exactly a confidence builder!

Well, true to his admonition, all rulings were going against me, and several times while on the record and off the record, he reminded me that he could always "refer the matter upstairs," a not-so-subtle reminder that the district attorney's office was two floors above. Finally, after about the third reminder, when I couldn't take it anymore, I ran the risk and responded, "You know, Judge, I'm tired of your blackmail. If you think that going to the D.A. will be of any benefit to these children, why don't you adjourn, go out that door, take the elevator, and do whatever you think is best." I'm a little fuzzy on his initial response, but I do remember that, whatever he said, my response was directed to the court reporter, to whom I said, "I want a copy of these minutes."

The judge's next words I do remember. He said, "If your client has money for the minutes, why doesn't he pay his wife what I recommended?"

My next response I will never forget: "He's not paying for the minutes, Judge, I am, so that I can refer this matter to where it belongs." I don't remember ever seeing a judge turn that color. He adjourned the trial until the next day and nearly fell as he got up and marched out the door to his chambers. That afternoon, the other attorney and I got together and worked out an agreement on the introduction of a ream of documents into evidence, since we both realized that this trial was going to last indefinitely. The next morning, when the judge took the bench, my adversary got up and told him of the agreement on the documents. You could have knocked me over with a feather when the judge said, "Well, Counselor, I'm glad to see that you and plaintiff's counsel have such a good relationship. I wish that he and I were on such good terms."

The rest of the trial went without incident, and lo and behold, the judge ruled on the money issue by awarding child support and maintenance in the same amounts that I had offered earlier. He then went on to advise each of the parties how lucky they both were to have attorneys dedicated to their respective cause. In his decision, he also inferred that both had been guilty of wrongdoing regarding the embezzled money.

I wish I could say that the parties then went their separate ways. No such luck. They continued to battle on several post-divorce issues, and when the IRS tax lien was levied, Beth refused to pay her share. Again, I failed to say no and had to make an application to be admitted into the tax court to try my one and only tax court case, which I, of course, won when the judge agreed that the finding in the matrimonial judgment was binding against Beth.

As I indicated earlier, by that time Beth and her first attorney, Simon, had become husband and wife.

It was about six years after the tax court trial, and it was a good thing that I was sitting down, when I received a call from Beth advising that she was going to divorce her husband Simon, and she asked whether I would represent her, since I had done such a good job representing Bill. I FINALLY LEARNED HOW TO SAY NO.

About two years after their divorce, I was saddened to learn that Simon had suddenly died of a heart attack, an occupational hazard.

Bill's second marriage lasted less than two years; the divorce proceeding about six years. Yes, I represented him, but that's another story.

Eagle Scout

In 2010, the Boy Scouts of America celebrated one hundred years of teaching the young men of our country the fundamentals of life, as set forth in their credo that a Boy Scout is trustworthy, loyal, helpful, friendly, courteous, kind, obedient, cheerful, thrifty, brave, clean, and reverent. It is these values, instilled in youth during their participation in Scouting, that help youth develop academic skills, self-confidence, ethics, leadership, and citizenship values that influence their adult lives.

At that time more than one in ten boys (11 percent) in the United States was a Scout, and an additional 23 percent became a Scout at some point in their lives. By the time boys reach adulthood, 54 percent have been in a Scouting program at some time in their youth. On average, 42 percent stay in Scouting for five or more years.

Scouting provides youth with an opportunity to try new things, provide service to others, build self-confidence, and reinforce ethical standards. These opportunities carry forward into their adult lives, improving their relationships, their work lives, their family lives, and the values by which they live. In fact, a Boy Scouts report found that 83 percent of men who were Scouts agree that the values they learned in Scouting continue to be very important to them today, with 63 percent who were Scouts five or more years strongly agreeing with this statement. Perhaps the Scout Oath says it best:

> "On my honor I will do my best to do my duty to God and my country and to obey the Scout Law; to help other people at all times; to keep myself physically strong, mentally awake, and morally straight."

The Eagle Scout is the highest advancement rank in Boy Scouting. In 2008, around 5 percent of all Boy Scouts earned the Eagle Scout rank. In 2008, the average age of boys earning the Eagle Scout rank was 17.3 years of age.

From 1912 to 2009, two million Boy Scouts earned the Eagle Scout rank. To earn the rank, a Boy Scout must progress through the ranks in the following order: Tenderfoot, Second Class, First Class, Star, Life, and Eagle. Twenty-one merit badges must be earned, including: First Aid, Citizenship in the Community, Citizenship in the Nation, Citizenship in the World, Communication, Environmental Science or Sustainability, Personal Fitness, Cooking, Camping, Family Life, Personal Management, Emergency Preparedness or Lifesaving, and Cycling, Hiking, or Swimming. The ultimate goal is membership in the National Eagle Scout Association.

It was in the late 1970s that Charles (Chuck) Leone came walking into my office along with his dad, Chuck Sr., and his mom, Eleanor. It took just a few moments to see the huge amount of respect, love, and affection the members of this family felt for one another. You could tell that this was a special young man. It is often the case that in like circumstances, the dad or mom will take over the conversation, leaving it to their child to fill in the blanks. In this instance, it was left to the son to explain the reason why the family had come to my office after being referred by a friend for whom I had recently recovered a large sum of money against a high school for injuries sustained by the friend.

During the one and a half hours that they were in the office, you could sense the terrible pain, both physical and mental, that young Chuck was in as he slowly but meticulously related his story.

It seemed that during the past summer, Chuck, an Eagle Scout, had attended two separate Scout camps. Unlike the usual Boy Scout camp, attended by Scouts going to camp along with their Scoutmaster and other members of their troupe, the camps attended by Chuck were camps attended for the purpose of earning certain merit badges. In this instance, the Scout or candidate would attend the camp, usually for one week, along with other Scouts seeking to earn the same merit badges, and while in attendance the group would be assigned to a provisional Scoutmaster who would see to it that they were safe, secure, well-fed, and in bed on time to be fresh for the next day's activities.

It seemed that Chuck, eager to earn the merit badges he wanted and needed, signed up for two separate merit badge camps that summer. Each was to begin on a Sunday but required that he arrive on Saturday to get settled in. Although it made for a tight schedule, these camps were set to begin on consecutive Sundays.

The first camp went by pretty much as scheduled, except for the fact that excessive rain delayed activities for almost a day. As a result, Chuck did not arrive at the second camp until Sunday, at about 1 P.M. Upon arrival, he was told where he would be bunking, he unpacked, put together a quick lunch, and had been left alone to fend for himself when he met two other Scouts who found themselves in similar circumstances.

Eager to make good use of their time, the three boys decided to go on a hike. After all, this was in the Catskill Mountains, and the mountains around them were so inviting. All in exceptionally good physical shape, they set out on their trek at about 2:15 P.M., intending to return by 4:30 P.M. They took off on a trail and soon found that they had probably ascended about one thousand feet. After resting in a clearing for about ten minutes, during which each ate a piece of fruit and took a drink of water, Chuck got up and left the clearing by himself, in order to relieve himself.

The sound that the other two boys reported hearing denoted a sense of danger and urgency. As if reading each other's mind, they both arose quickly and moved in the direction that Chuck had gone. After carefully moving through the underbrush, it was Frank Lacy who first saw what had occurred as he looked down from the edge of a cliff about twenty-five feet to where Chuck lay, writhing in pain. As quickly as they could, Frank and Steve Johnson lowered themselves down into the ravine where Chuck had fallen.

Upon arriving at the side of their fallen friend, they both made use of their first aid skills to determine the extent of Chuck's injuries. Once they were satisfied that there appeared to be no broken bones, they allowed Chuck to collect himself, then helped him up into a sitting position and slowly onto his feet. Although he was still in pain, Chuck declined the offer that one of them go back to base camp for a stretcher, and they began to walk slowly back to their barracks. As they walked, each expressed concern that they could be in trouble for going off on their own. They worried that they would be sent home, unable to finish camp and earn their merit badges. For better or worse, they decided not to tell anyone about their misadventure. The shock was wearing off; the adrenalin was easing the pain; and the thought of being able to carry on a secret plan actually caused them to chuckle as they approached the barracks. The plan was simple. Chuck would get into his bunk and act as if he had just arrived and was tired when they met the provisional Scoutmaster. Frank and Steve would bring a meal to Chuck from the informal dinner planned for that evening. Chuck would take aspirin supplied from their first aid kits as needed, and they would hope for the best by morning. If necessary, one of them would answer "present" on Chuck's behalf at roll call when attendance was taken, and they would then play it by ear.

The plan went well until the following late afternoon, when Chuck's back pain became intolerable. Realizing that Chuck needed assistance, the three boys walked to the infirmary.

Only Chuck went inside, at which time he told the nurse about the fall and his continued back pain. The nurse, after taking his vital signs and examining him, admitted him into the infirmary for observation. Following twenty-four hours of bed rest, and after questioning Chuck, who reported an easing of his symptoms, the nurse released Chuck from the infirmary and handed him a sealed envelope, with instructions to give the envelope to the provisional Scoutmaster upon his return to the barracks, which he did. Having eaten in the infirmary before he left, Chuck, who was once again sore after the walk, lay down and went to sleep, not waking again until the next morning. His friends brought him breakfast, after which he did manage to make it to the attendance lineup and then through the activities of the day, which luckily did not involve much physical activity.

Five more days, and it would all be over. Chuck missed one more morning lineup and two more afternoon lineups; was able to fake it through physical activities, although still in pain; and successfully made it through to the end of camp and the bus ride home.

Chuck was only home for about two hours when his dad came home, saw him move around, and asked him what was wrong. Chuck told his mom and dad everything that had happened. Chuck's dad, a former Air Force pilot before beginning work for a major commercial airline and eventually becoming its chief mechanic, was outraged, not only at his son, but by the lack of supervision that the Scouts had exhibited. Chuck had studiously followed his dad's advice, hoping to become an Air Force cadet, following in the footsteps of his dad. The young man was immediately taken to the family orthopedist, who after extensive examination and testing, reported that Chuck had sustained three compression fractures of the lower spine. The proper care after such injury is four to six weeks of complete bed rest. While the doctor put Chuck on immediate bed rest, the week that Chuck spent at camp could prove insurmountable to a complete recovery. Only time would tell.

It was only after his bed rest was complete and he had received clearance from the doctor that Chuck, his mom, and his dad came in to see me. After hearing the story, I told them that I had to do two key things before deciding whether to take on the case. The first was to question the two other boys, one at a time. Separate interviews were needed so that each could tell his own story. The next was to make a trip to the camp so that I could see where the accident occurred with my own eyes. It has been my experience that since accidents are not expected to occur and sometimes happen within the blink of an eye and at times of stress, clients are the worst relayers of information. The trouble was that there had already been a change in the foliage, but any firsthand inspection was better than nothing. The two boys (with permission of their parents), along with Chuck's dad and I, made the trip and climbed to the location of the accident.

Even then, it took much soul-searching to decide whether to take the case. Although I was convinced that there was a good, meritorious case, suing the Boy Scouts is like defiling the American flag. And it was a challenge since I would only get paid if I won. The time would be considerable and the cost of developing the case expensive. The counterbalancing argument was that everyone is entitled to be represented by an attorney. The fact that I also had been a Scout figured in. All in all, to refuse to take on this challenge would make me wonder if I really had it in me to be one of the best. It is a fact that the best trial attorneys lose more cases than the worst because they are willing to take on the most difficult cases. It's like in baseball. Sometimes the fielder who wins the Golden Glove Award is not really the best fielder. In baseball, if the fielder doesn't touch the ball, the official scorer will not give him an error. Sometimes the fielder with the greatest range will reach a ball that others could not get near, only to have an error called when his throw to first base goes awry. Given all this, would I take the case? Yes, I would, I proudly decided, to the delight of my clients.

Somewhat surprisingly, neither the Boy Scouts nor their insurance company had reached out to Chuck for a statement or with an offer to pay his medical bills. So instead of serving a claims letter, which would put the Scouts on notice of a potential claim, I decided to waste no time and served a summons and complaint upon the Boy Scouts entity that owned and managed the campgrounds. The theories set forth were based upon negligent management and supervision of the campsite, maintaining dangerous areas therein, and nursing malpractice for not properly caring for Chuck and/or referring him to a hospital for proper care and treatment. I was somewhat surprised to learn in their answer, as well as in an initial telephone conference with their attorneys, that the Boy Scouts claimed the summons and complaint constituted their first awareness that an accident had occurred. It was only later, during the phase of litigation known as pretrial discovery, that I learned the alleged reason for this position. When I took the deposition of the nurse, Ms. Lawless, she denied, under oath, that Chuck told her of the fall from the cliff. The only entry in the infirmary logbook was that Chuck complained of a headache; she found him to have a fever and kept him overnight, releasing him the next day when the fever broke. She produced the logbook, in which she identified the writing to be hers. She also testified about the procedure of giving a sealed envelope to the Scout for transmittal to the provisional Scoutmaster. She denied keeping a copy of the note or any knowledge of its whereabouts. Her testimony was based upon the accuracy of the records, which the rules of evidence allowed her to do since she said she had no current recollection of the events.

The camp director who was deposed also denied that the accident had been reported and further denied that any portion of the camp used for hiking was in any way dangerous. The court refused my request to depose the executive director of the Boy Scouts, in effect accepting the notion that this claim lacked merit and was a waste of the court's time as well as the time of the Boy Scouts, which would be better served in carrying on their virtuous benefit to society.

Why, you might ask, did I continue to believe in the truth of my client's claim? To disbelieve not only him but also Frank and Steve was simply not something I could countenance. These boys, to me, represented the best that our future had to offer. They were civic-minded, brilliant students, and I was sure they would become leaders of their community. Chuck's ambition was to serve his country in the Air Force. On the other hand, I simply could not accept the notion that the Boy Scouts were collectively conspiring to lie about Chuck's injury. Chuck's chosen career was now in jeopardy since it was uncertain whether he would ever sufficiently recover to enable him to pass the physical exam necessary to receive a commission in the Air Force Academy.

The orthopedist who treated Chuck assured his dad that the delay in treatment and failure to refer Chuck immediately to a hospital had a significant effect upon the permanent disability he was sure to be left with. When I received his medical report, however, I was dismayed to find that the orthopedist said in the report that he couldn't state with a reasonable degree of medical certainty that the delay had an effect on the outcome. All attempts by me or by Chuck's dad to discuss this with the doctor fell on deaf ears. Finally, only after speaking to the parish priest of the church that the doctor and Chuck's father belonged to, did the doctor relent and send us a new report stating that the delay did affect the outcome, which we immediately served upon our adversary. It was with the feeling of being a one-armed fighter that we picked a jury and commenced the trial.

I make it a practice to always know who is sitting in the courtroom, as I do have the right to ask that any potential witness be excused from the courtroom. I quickly learned that the gentleman sitting there right from the beginning to the end of the trial was a representative of the insurance company that covered the Boy Scouts—the company that would be on the hook in the event that we won.

I put the two boys on the stand, and they recounted the events as they remembered them. Then, feeling that I had no choice but to shoot from the hip, I called to the stand the executive director of the Boy Scouts, the same person I wanted to examine earlier in the pretrial phase, a request denied by the court. The reason I say shoot from the hip is that an attorney should never ask a question he does not know the answer to, especially if the witness is aligned with the opposition. However, it turned out to be a good strategy because finally there was a crack in the wall of the Boy Scouts' defense. The executive director, Mr. Chancellor, was a career member of the U.S. diplomatic corps and was assigned to our United Nations delegation. After repeating that the Boy Scouts were unaware of the accident until they received the summons and complaint, he did testify that if the boys were allowed to go on an unsupervised hike, that was against policy and never should have been allowed. He also testified that if the accident happened in the location claimed, there were dangerous spots in that section. Sensing that my instincts were correct and that we had a shot at winning, I assigned the best investigator money could buy to find the provisional Scoutmaster. In the meantime, I put Nurse Lawless on the stand. She repeated her deposition testimony that Chuck said nothing about a fall, and on cross-examination, the defendant's attorney offered into evidence the infirmary logbook. Chuck was the next to take the stand, and I could not have been prouder of him as he testified on direct and stood up to a withering cross-examination by the defendant's attorney, who accused him of being an outright liar.

The next to take the stand was a charming professor of nursing, whose testimony was direct and to the point. She opined that, assuming Chuck's testimony was true, the camp nurse was guilty of nursing malpractice. Cross-examination was short and ineffectual.

With great trepidation, I then called Chuck's treating physician to the stand and, although it was a struggle, I was able to get the testimony I needed to establish that Chuck's treatment constituted medical malpractice and that the delay in treatment affected the outcome. The cross-examination, however, was a nightmare. Untrue to his word, the doctor had not destroyed his original report when I returned it to him, so when his file was subpoenaed by the court, in it was the original of his first report, along with the copy of his second report, the one I had served upon my adversary. I truly believe that I did not breathe as the doctor gave his explanation for the two reports, with the differing opinions on the delay in treatment, which, fortunately, the judge allowed the doctor to give in narrative form. The doctor testified that six years prior, he had suffered a heart attack. The advice given by his doctor was for him to avoid stressful situations. Three times before the heart attack, he had the occasion to testify at a trial for one of his patients, and he found the experience of being questioned on cross-examination by an aggressive attorney, who attacked his professionalism and veracity, to be the most stressful experience he ever had. He went on to testify that if he gave us the opinion we sought, he was sure he would be called on to testify; to avoid that probability, he said, he had lied in the first report. It was only after the parish priest sought him out, at the request of Chuck's father, that he realized the wrong he had done and wrote the revised report. The last portion of the testimony was given as the doctor sat sobbing, at times uncontrollably, on the stand. The defense lawyer, stunned, asked nothing further. Thank God it was lunchtime, as I did not know whether to laugh or cry. I later discovered that the jury believed every word. I suppose it's true that "the truth will set you free."

No sooner had the dust settled than I got word that my investigator had located the provisional Scoutmaster, who was now an undercover agent with the Drug Enforcement Administration. When I explained why I needed him as a witness to the U.S. Attorney's Office, the best I could get was an agreement that the DEA would produce him in two days but that I could not interview him because they would not pull him out of the field twice. Since beggars can't be choosers, I agreed, and as promised, in a suit and tie, as if from central casting, in came the agent. Again, I had to shoot from the hip, asking questions, even though I did not know how he would answer. After establishing his identity, his current employment, and that he was the provisional Scoutmaster at the time of the incident, I asked him whether he knew of my client. He explained that he remembered that Chuck was an Eagle Scout who had arrived on a Sunday, a day late, and was assigned to him but whom he did not meet until the following evening when Chuck introduced himself. He explained that Chuck had been in the infirmary and had given him a sealed envelope from the nurse, which was the camp's custom and practice. I will never forget his words when I asked him if he remembered what was in the note. He matter-of-factly said, "Well, it would help if I had the note in front of me."

When I explained that the Boy Scouts denied having the note, his response was, "Well, it would help if I could go to my attaché case."

When I asked why, he said, "Well, I have the note." At these words, everyone in the courtroom gasped.

With the permission of the court, he got up, walked to the seat where he had left his attaché case, opened it, and after removing a sheet of paper, returned to the witness stand. "May I see the note?" was my next question, and the court officer took it from the witness and handed it to me. Needing to lay what is known as a "proper foundation" to eventually put the document in evidence, I next asked, "Agent, isn't this a photostatic copy of the note?" When he said yes, I had the copy marked for identification only, and then I asked him for the original because, under what is known as the "best evidence rule," I had to establish why the original was not being offered.

Once again, his response was, "It would be best if I went back to my attaché case," which he was allowed to do, and again he came back to the stand with another document, which, upon request, was given to me by the court officer.

I returned it to the witness and asked him, "Where is the original of this note?" Using the document, which at that point was marked for identification only, he went on to testify: "After camp was over, I had a feeling that something might come out of this, so I made a copy of the note and I sent it, along with a copy of this letter, explaining whatever I knew to the Boy Scouts, along with a copy to their insurance company." My next question was whether he had sent it to anyone's attention. "Yes," he said, as he looked at the letter to refresh his recollection, and he went on to name the very camp director who had testified at his deposition and at the trial that the Boy Scouts knew nothing about the accident until receipt of the summons and complaint. With respect to the insurance company, he testified that the copy went to the attention of the same insurance representative who had sat in at the trial since its beginning, and he pointed him out to the jury.

I then, in the most dramatic way possible, got up and demanded that the attorney turn over the original note and letter, which he of course denied having. All of this satisfied the "best evidence rule," putting me in the position to offer the copy of the note into evidence, which the judge permitted over the objection of the defense attorney. I then was in the position to request that the agent read the content of the note to the jury, a moment which I consider to be one of the best of my career. The agent, staring at the jury, read aloud: "Chuck Leone came to infirmary in the P.M., complaining of back pain after fall from a cliff. Kept overnight until following P.M. when the pain subsided. Given aspirin and allowed to return to bunk. If pain continues, to be returned to infirmary for transfer to hospital." It was signed by Nurse Lawless, who had testified at her deposition and at the trial that Chuck never told anyone about the accident. I then offered the copy of the agent's letter into evidence, but the judge sustained the defense counsel's objection; why, I don't know, but who cared? The damage was done. The DEA agent went back undercover after my profuse thanks, a handshake, and a hug.

We adjourned for lunch, but fatigued and with my mind racing, I asked permission to stay in the courtroom over the lunch break, which was granted. When the court reconvened, the defense counsel got up and, for whatever the reason, advised the judge that he was withdrawing his objection to the introduction into evidence of the agent's letter, probably because it referenced certain activities that Chuck was able to participate in after the accident. My response was, "It's too late, Judge," and I went on to explain that since the letter was marked only for identification, it was given back to the DEA agent, who was now gone and unavailable.

The defense counsel's next move borders on the unbelievable. He got up and said, "I'll offer my copy, Judge."

"What copy?" I yelled at the top of my lungs, knowing that the agent left without any copy having been made. Then I added: "When does the district attorney get involved, Judge?" I truly believe that, realizing the box the defendant's attorney had put himself in, the judge recessed and brought all the attorneys into his chambers only to get things calmed down.

"This is a civil trial for money. No one's going to jail. You're ahead of the game, counsel," he said, looking at me. "Let's have summations tomorrow and put this baby to sleep."

The next morning, after defense summation, the judge, wanting the case to go to the jury that day, adjourned for a shortened lunch period, to resume at 1 P.M. instead of the normal time of 2 P.M. The defense counsel, always the gamesman, did not show up until 2 P.M., claiming he had misunderstood. I now know what it is like to be a football field goal kicker when the other side asks for a time out just to let the kicker think about the upcoming game-winning or game-losing kick. Collecting my nerves and realizing that I could not attack the Boy Scouts as an institution, I nevertheless attacked those representatives who had wrapped themselves in our flag and implied that Chuck and his friend had violated every principle for which Scouting stands. Without sufficient time to instruct the jury on the law, the judge was forced to take the unusual action of adjourning until the next court day, a Monday. Little matter, because in the end, the jury gave the defendant Boy Scouts the drubbing they deserved.

Chuck did go on to become an aeronautical engineer and a private pilot, but he was unable to serve in the military as he so wanted to do. One of the other boys is a doctor, and one is an attorney. From beginning to end, the case lasted about three years. I'm sure that it took ten years off my life, but hey, what's great about being a trial lawyer is that you learn something new every day.

Courtrooms are open to the public, and the show is free. If you go to watch a trial and one of the lawyers asks who you are, maybe he was trained by me.

English—Who Needs English?

It was 1969 when the controversy arose.

The assassination of Martin Luther King Jr. on April 4, 1968, had caused riots in the streets of many major cities around the country. Racial hysteria was the issue of the day. People were afraid to leave their homes. Police were working double time and sometimes triple time to maintain order. Many departments were understaffed, and minorities were underrepresented. In a number of locales, civil service promotional exams were years behind schedule. Cities had been turned into ruins, and there had been loss of life and people injured so often that newspapers regularly contained daily casualty reports.

It was in this charged atmosphere that the city with the largest police department in the country, New York, desperately in need of change and restaffing, conducted its long-overdue promotional exam for advancement from the rank of lieutenant to captain. With the department staffed entirely by civil service personnel, civil service rules naturally applied to the exam. While there were review courses offered by many entities, most candidates studied by reading review books published by the Arco Publishing Company. These books were readily available in bookstores and on the used-book market, sold by prior candidates who had already advanced in rank. It was not uncommon to find questions and answers that had appeared on prior exams administered in the city, the state, and other jurisdictions throughout the country. It must be noted that this material was released by those administering these exams and not wrongly obtained by Arco.

So, when word started spreading like wildfire that a court proceeding had been commenced in the New York State Supreme Court seeking to invalidate the entire exam, there was no bigger news item under discussion. It did not come as a surprise that our firm, with the Commish (a former New York City deputy police commissioner) at the helm, was consulted. What did come as a surprise was the number of lieutenants who had come together to form a group seeking to have the case thrown out of court. One hundred thirty-nine police lieutenants, from the regular police department, the housing police department, and the transit police department, all confident that they had scored high enough on the exam to deserve promotion to captain, had banded together as brothers. They were stunned that the court had granted a Temporary Restraining Order delaying the Civil Service Department from grading the exam and calling upon the chiefs of police to show cause why the entire exam should not be voided. It was the grounds upon which this challenge was brought that shocked the civil service community. Those grounds were that in the multiple-choice portion of the exam were twelve English grammar questions, taken in the order they appeared from a California civil service exam held twelve years prior to the New York City exam, and that all of the questions and answers had appeared in an Arco publication that was first printed about four years before this exam.

For some, to study for the exam was no more difficult than following a recipe to bake a cake. For others who had long ago graduated from the Police Academy, the test presented a difficult challenge. In addition to working overtime, sometimes moonlighting at a second job, and also fulfilling their obligations as a husband and father, it was grueling experience. Just the tension of fighting for that extra pay could be demanding.

Still, they were certain of their successful performance, so it was not a surprise that each member of the group was willing to put up a $100 retainer and agree to a further fee of $1,000, contingent on the success of our firm in arguing that the exam should not be invalidated. Our firm, equally certain of success, was willing to run the risk for a minimum retainer. Sometimes you just have to let it roll.

After performing exhaustive research and creating well-prepared papers in support of our petition, we marched into court, ready to do battle at the oral argument. Thank goodness all of the men and women who came to court to support their position, either pro or con, were prepared to accept the rule of law. Otherwise, I realized, there was enough firepower in that courtroom to make the famous shootout at the O.K. Corral seem like a cake sale.

The essence of the oral argument put forth by the attorney for Lieutenant Hardman, whose complaint had challenged the validity of the promotional exam, was that he had not read the Arco publication containing these twelve true-or-false questions pertaining to the proper use of the English language, and that, as a member of the black community, he and test-takers such as him, who did not attend the "better schools," were at a marked disadvantage. Since the tests had not been graded at that point, one can only assume that the lieutenant thought he had gotten these answers wrong, but this could only be speculated upon.

In opposition, we submitted proof that the lieutenant, in fact, was raised in a privileged community and had attended a private parochial high school.

The presiding judge reserved decision, and after about three weeks, issued his decision and order, vacating the temporary stay and finding in our favor, determining that the understanding of the English language was an integral part of the work of a police officer and that the Arco publication was available on the open market and therefore presented no significant advantage to anyone. He also noted that there was no direct proof that any of our 139 petitioners had seen the publication. He added that it was the usual practice of this and other civil service agencies to include prior exams from almost any venue in preparing these types of exams. If we had written the decision ourselves, it could not have been better composed for our side.

The celebration was short-lived, though. We soon received an Order to Show Cause, signed by an appellate division judge, along with a Notice of Appeal staying the grading of the exam until an appeal could be heard in the Appellate Division (the intermediate appeals court in the state) reviewing the decision and order of the judge.

Although the appeal was to be handled on an expedited schedule, it would be months before a decision. Morale in the department could not have been worse, as those who thought they had passed were, to say the least, miffed at those who joined with Lieutenant Hardman, believing that they had not performed well on the test and wanting to see it thrown out for any reason.

We were confident in our position, so it came as no shock that the Appellate Division unanimously affirmed the lower-court decision. Now, could we put the champagne on ice, please? Again, NO! In came the Order to Show Cause signed by a judge from the Court of Appeals (the highest appellate court in the state) again staying the grading of the exam until our opposition could convince that court that the case was of significant import to warrant the Court of Appeals hearing the case. Having lost on both lower-court levels any appeal was not a matter of right but could be taken only if the Court of Appeals said so. I must admit that it rattled our cage when the order came down that the Court of Appeals had agreed to hear the case. What really was troubling was the feedback that the Commish got when he reached out to his political cronies. It seemed that through back channels, discussions were going on between the local and state politicos who were concerned that a ruling in our favor could trigger another race riot, since news coverage of the case always seemed to include the subject of race.

When the case came up for oral argument in the Court of Appeals, the news coverage was extreme. Given the outside issues and political overtones, the Commish was the right choice to present the oral argument on our behalf. A leading activist/attorney appeared for the other side. Sticking solely to the issues, our argument was direct and to the point. We were somewhat surprised that our adversary's argument did not stray too much from the issues either. Perhaps this tactic should have been a harbinger of bad news to come because it took only about a week for the Court of Appeals to issue its decision, reversing both lower courts and throwing out the entire civil service exam as tainted by the inclusion of the twelve English questions.

There are no words to describe our dismay when our backdoor contacts made it unequivocally clear that the local government's plea to prevent a race riot won out over the rule of law. As far as we were concerned, the opposition had blackmailed its way to victory.

I am proud to say that our firm was not willing to give up and just "play the game." I welcomed being asked to take on the task of attacking the decision of the Court of Appeals. My job would be to make a motion for re-argument. My tactic was to take apart the decision of the court, word for word, in support of my belief that the court had used such general language in its decision (I believe to hide the real reason for the ruling) that the decision would or could endanger every civil service exam in the future.

For example, the use of questions from any prior examination, a time-tested technique, might be subject to attack in the future by reason of the court's poorly worded decision.

Apparently, my approach worked. There is a treatise on the Court of Appeals, authored by Henry Cohen and Arthur Karger, that is considered the bible when it comes to New York Court of Appeals practice and history. My research supported my assertion that this was the only time in its history that the New York State Court of Appeals vacated its entire decision and directed that a new oral argument be held on a date set in its decision. Having won the battle, however, I still had to win the war.

So intense were our clients that when the new oral argument was set for a Friday morning, three armed lieutenants came to my home on Thursday morning and were assigned to escort me upstate to the Court of Appeals, to guard me at dinner and overnight, and to safely deposit me in the courtroom the next day. This was not my first appearance at that court, but it was the first time I felt like General Patton leading an army to war.

I generally believe that the questions put to me and my adversary by all of the judges demonstrated that this time around they appeared to be interested in deciding the case on its merits, but looks can be deceiving. It was about two-thirds of the way through the arguments when one of the judges asked me a question that still troubles me to this day. "Counselor," he said, "suppose we simply eliminate the twelve English questions and mark the rest of the exam. How would you feel about that?"

For about twenty seconds, my mind ran like a computer, trying to figure out all the possibilities and odds, and then the only answer I could give came out: "Your Honor, I represent one hundred and thirty-nine clients, all of whom believe they scored well enough to earn their promotion. Depending on how well any of them did on the twelve English questions, elimination of these questions might result in a candidate going up, or maybe down, in ranking. If I agreed with your idea, I might be arguing in opposition to the interests of one of my clients. I must therefore respectfully decline to answer your question except to say that I continue to propound the position that the entire exam be graded." The judge complimented me for my analysis.

In a five-to-two decision, using more carefully chosen words, the court affirmed its original decision and voided the entire exam.

I am happy to say that almost all of our group, after taking the next promotional exam, eventually became captains, and some went on to earn higher ranking.

As for Lieutenant Hardman, about one-and-a-half years later, he was charged with accepting bribe money and was thrown off the force, forfeiting all pension benefits. He claimed it was a setup because he was hated by fellow officers. They say what goes around comes around.

Should I have answered differently? I'll let you be the judge.

From the Absurd to the Sublime

The events in this story started to unfold in 1975. It is necessary, however, to take you back more than forty years in order to have a full appreciation of these events.

After graduating from law school in 1931, my client was offered a position with the State Prosecutor's Office, now known as the District Attorney's Office. After two years, he left because he had always wanted to be in private practice. That proved to be a mistake because the Depression turned out to be the worst time to go into private practice. However, he was involved in local politics and served as a precinct captain in his district, which helped him to become a court officer. Although it was not a high-paying job, it offered the security of a regular paycheck, along with other fringe benefits, and kept him off the soup line, which so many unemployed Americans depended upon for their daily sustenance. This was supposed to be a temporary job, an escape from the Depression until the economy improved so that he could go back to private practice. Well, it didn't turn out that way. Marriage, a baby in 1938, modest yearly raises, the prospect of a pension down the line, the drawn-out Depression, followed by an austere World War II economy kept the dream of private practice always out of reach.

After about six years on the job, one of the new Superior Court judges, who was later to be a state Supreme Court judge under a statewide court reorganization, took a liking to him and arranged to have him appointed as the judge's personal court attaché. Still in uniform, this meant that he always worked in that judge's courtroom or chambers. It also meant a step up in pay and an increase in his pay grade. In those days, each judge had a staff of four employees permanently assigned to him; a secretary/typist, a legal secretary who advised him on the law and helped with legal research, a legal assistant, and the court attaché. Over time, as each retired, my client moved up the chain. These job advances, combined with yearly raises, increasing pension and health benefits, the security of a civil service job, plus the birth of a second child lessened the disappointment of not being in private practice. Also, once he became the legal assistant, he was allowed to perform legal services on his own time, as long as they did not lead to litigation, which the rules did not permit him to do. With that extra money, he and his family lived comfortably, but they would never be rich. Eventually, the dream of private practice dimmed, replaced by the hope that someday, his continued political involvement might lead to an appointed judgeship. Since retirement and pension benefits are calculated on years in civil service and a percentage of your last year's pay, that judgeship loomed in the distance like a pot of gold at the end of a rainbow. If I can retire on that pension at a young enough age, I can then go into private practice, he reasoned. The thought that large firms are always looking for retired judges to add to their mastheads only served to enhance the dream, which, although dimmed, never faded away.

Finally, thirty years after admission to the Bar, he became the legal secretary—hopefully, the steppingstone he needed. By this time, the judge he had spent about twenty years with had risen to be the senior judge. Also, after the court reorganization, the law secretaries were given the option of joining the executive pension system, which they elected to do because it offered a better pension upon retirement. The fly in the ointment was that politics is a dirty system; the concept of fairness has never been one of its strong points. It seemed that the Democratic Party leader wanted the judge to appoint someone else to the position of law secretary. Either out of a sense of loyalty or because my client threatened to retire, the judge decided to buck the party and appointed my client. This decision virtually assured several things: Appointment of my client to a judgeship was out. The judge lost the opportunity to serve three additional two-year extensions upon reaching the age of seventy since those appointments were dependent upon party endorsement. And the client had to separate himself from party involvement. The deal struck was that the client would not retire until the judge turned seventy, when the judge would be forced to retire. So, after more than forty years of service at this "short-time civil service job," my client, in early 1975, filed his Notice of Retirement and his application for pension benefits, to take effect thirty days thereafter. This is where I come in and the legal story begins.

In the pension application, my client applied for accumulated vacation time and terminal leave. Utilizing the tables furnished, these combined accumulated benefits, based upon his forty-plus years in service, totaled almost $240,000 in addition to his monthly pension. The response he received was a request to furnish his time records for all years of service. The problem was that when he began, no time records were kept, since none were required. It was not until the law secretaries voted to join the Executive Pay Plan in the early 1960s that time records were kept for all court employees. The accumulated records that were kept were submitted, along with an explanation about the missing years. The response was that the absence of complete time records was still a problem. The judge then submitted an affidavit to the effect that the applicant, to the best of his recollection, was never absent in excess of the sick days allowed. Again, the application was denied, with cautionary language that the comptroller would do its own calculation if actual time records were not submitted within fourteen days.

I was then hired to represent not only this client but also two other law secretaries who were in the same boat. I commenced an action known as an Article 78 Proceeding against the agency responsible, known as the Office of Court Administration, which governs all of the courts within the five boroughs in the city of New York. This is the type of legal action necessary to review conduct of an administrative agency to determine whether its actions or determinations have been arbitrary or capricious. It contains, in addition to the affidavits and other proof, a Notice of Petition, affording the respondent agency the time required by law to answer the petition and fixing a date known as the return date, the day on which the proceeding will come up for mandatory oral argument. The judge scheduled to hear and decide the proceeding would be the judge who, at that time, was the judge who presided in Special Term, Part I, where all motions and Special Proceedings were calendared for oral argument. Contained in the respondent's answering papers, along with the defensive arguments, was something called an Affirmative Defense, in which, without stating the reason, the respondent Office of Court Administration requested a change of venue, asking that the proceeding be moved to another Supreme Court remote from the court in which the proceeding was brought, which, by court rule, was the same court in which all the events had occurred.

The transcript of the oral argument was so memorable that, in my opinion, it should be displayed in a museum housing court memorabilia and other artifacts. At the oral argument, after I presented my side of the case and the respondent lawyer stood up, the judge directed that the first thing he address was the request for a change of venue. This proceeding had attracted much attention, so the large courtroom was standing room only, filled with attorneys and the media.

All were stunned when the lawyer responded with his position: "Your Honor," he stated, "it is the position of the Office of Court Administration that, given the length of time that these petitioners have worked in this courthouse, my client cannot get a fair trial, and therefore this case should be moved upstate to a courthouse located in our state's capital, where justice can best be served." Taken aback by this unheard of application and the tumult it created in the courtroom, the judge called a recess and directed that further argument be adjourned until he could consult with the administrative judge. He simply was stunned and had no idea what to do. That conference was held in the chambers of the administrative judge with all attorneys present, including the judge from Special Term, Part I.

Shaken by the difficult decision he faced, the administrative judge nonetheless came up with an idea that seemed workable. The only thing that caused me to wonder about his choice was whether he had spoken directly with his boss, the Office of Court Administration, before the conference. That I will never know. His suggestion was to adjourn the case for four weeks and assign it to another judge. In those days, a schedule of assignments to the various court parts was prepared at the beginning of the calendar year and available to all attorneys. Looking at this "Red Book," we all knew the names of the judges assigned for the next three months. During the fourth week from the conference, the judge sitting in the motion part was was an acting Supreme Court judge, a lesser-grade

Civil Court judge assigned to sit in the Supreme Court. It was an honorary position that quite often led to a permanent seat on the Supreme Court, along with the substantial pay raise that the permanent position offered. The rationale in considering this judge was that he did not have a history of interaction with any of the petitioners, the expressed concern of the respondent. The downside was that an acting Supreme Court judge, seeking that promotion, might not have the moxie to rule against the very agency that held his future in its hands. It was a tough call, but for a number of reasons, some of which I shall relate, we decided that this judge, who had a reputation of honesty and integrity, could sit impartially and rule in a just and legal manner. So the oral argument was adjourned for four weeks, when the agreed-upon judge would be sitting in the motion part and hear oral argument.

I entered the courthouse that day on shaky legs, having been unable to sleep much the night before. The standing-room-only crowd did nothing to calm my nerves. When the case was called, I thought I was going to vomit as I started to make my presentation. I had only gotten about ten words into my presentation when the judge interrupted and said, "Counselor, I've read all the papers. Counsel for the Respondent, if I understand your position, your client is demanding records that were not required under petitioner's original pay plan; required only when they elected to switch to the Executive Pay Plan, which they have furnished. I'm a baseball fan. Explain to me how this is any different than changing the rules of the game after the fifth inning, and you better make it good, and you better answer to the point." Stunned, the attorney hemmed and hawed for about twenty seconds, at which point the judge again warned him to answer the question. When he was unable to do so, the judge told him to sit down and then proceeded to issue his ruling from the bench, not waiting to issue it under less public circumstances. He announced his decision in favor of the petitioners, awarding court costs and interest to boot.

My original client, after collecting his money, took the Florida Bar Exam, which he had prepared for in advance of retiring, and passed on the first attempt. The Florida Board of Bar Examiners then denied his application for admission to the Florida Bar. Conditions for admission included graduation from an accredited law school or ten years of active practice. They ruled that the Florida statute meant that the law school had to be accredited at the time of graduation. Since the law school from which he had graduated was not accredited until twenty years after his graduation, they found that he would have to satisfy the "ten years of active practice" rule. In their opinion, his position as law secretary for the senior judge of the State Supreme Court did not constitute active practice.

"Northerners need not apply" was the clear underlying message. After producing an extensive list of his personal client files, together with an affidavit from the judge and a letter from the appellate court outlining a list of special projects he had worked on, he again failed to meet the state Bar's requirements. It was only after I commenced a Special Proceeding directly with the state's highest appellate court that the Florida Board of Bar Examiners was directed to admit my client to the Florida Bar without further delay.

By then a resident of Florida, which was also a requirement, he became the oldest attorney to gain acceptance to the Florida Bar in the state's history, gaining admission at the age of seventy-six. Living out his dream, he actively practiced law for the better part of seven years before Parkinson's disease quickly ravaged his body. With great sorrow, he sent a letter to the Bar, voluntarily resigning due to his health. Three weeks after sending that letter, and six days after entering a nursing home, he passed away in his sleep, leaving his wife and two children to survive him. All believe that he died a happy man after living long enough to fulfill his lifetime dream of private practice—more than forty years late, but better late than never. In a way, that dream was fulfilled by proxy when his son became an attorney and thrived for many years in private practice. That client, you see, was my father.

He Was Crazy for His Wife

When Tom Zuski first walked into my office, other than the fact that he was clearly still in pain from a car accident, there was nothing else about him that would indicate the amount of trouble he would cause me during the following two years. I first met him in the hospital a few days after his accident, having been recommended by a co-worker of Tom's who had once been my client. He worked for an architectural firm as a draftsman and had been at the firm for several years, earning a yearly salary of about $65,000. His car had been hit from the rear, causing him to sustain a lower-back injury involving three spinal discs, and he had no prior injury or pain in that area. The work as a draftsman required that he lean over the drafting table while seated and bent forward, a position that even a young man might have found difficult. Tom was in his early fifties and clearly this injury, if it did not heal correctly, had the potential to end his career.

I learned that he and his wife had both immigrated to this country as adults after World War II from a country in Eastern Europe that no longer exists. All other family members had been lost during the war. Although to this day I have never met Mrs. Zuski, she also became a client, since she was entitled to maintain a derivative cause of action, or secondary claim, because of her husband's injury. He signed his retainer while I was with him in the hospital. She sent hers back through the mail. I also learned that Mrs. Zuski had been a psychiatrist in her native country and that, after a few years of additional training in the United States, she earned her degree in psychiatry and was licensed in New York State. She worked at a state-run mental health facility where she had been employed for several years. She apparently was hardworking and put in many long hours to earn overtime. As a result, I was never able to meet her in person, although I tried.

The first thing I did after being retained was to apply for the no-fault benefits, which anyone involved in a car accident must do if they are injured or out of work. With these benefits, medical and hospital bills are paid for, and the injured is entitled to 80 percent of lost earnings, up to a maximum of $2,500 per month at that time, regardless of how much more was earned. For an additional premium, you can apply for additional lost-wage benefits, up to $5,000 per month, if in fact 80 percent of your salary equals or exceeds that amount. At that time, no-fault insurance was relatively new. It added a tremendous amount of paperwork and, in effect, lowered the value of a negligence case, since basic lost earnings and medical expenses no longer were included in the claim for monetary damages because they were no longer out of pocket. Negligence case retainers were regulated by statute. For the past thirty years, the retainer had to be contingent on recovery and could be taken in only one of two ways in the case of an adult. It could be a sliding scale, which started out at 50 percent of the first thousand dollars of recovery and worked its way down to 25 percent of any recovery exceeding $25,000. Or it could be a straight one-third of any recovery, which was the retainer of choice by the attorney if it was expected that the recovery would exceed $35,000. Usually, there was a great deal of extra work involved in trying to separate a large amount of money from the octopus known as a liability insurance company.

There was no provision in the statute that regulated whether the attorney was allowed to charge for the additional, often complex work necessary to process the client's claim for no-fault benefits. Most attorneys at the time were charging a flat fee of 10 percent of the lost-wage benefits for work involving no-fault benefits of any kind, although some attorneys of a lower stature, desperate for work, were doing it for free, since other aspects of no-fault law requiring that a qualifying injury be sustained before you could sue were having the effect of reducing the number of lawsuits that could be brought.

For the first several months, when Tom's lost-wage check for $2,500 would come in, I deducted my 10 percent and remitted the rest to him. A lawsuit had been instituted on their behalf. It was only during a conversation with the no-fault adjuster that I learned for the first time that Tom had paid the additional premium and that he was entitled to $5,000 per month. I fought for and obtained the back money that was due, close to $8,500, prorated for part of a month, and remitted the money due to the client. It was Mrs. Zuski who complained, feeling that my share should remain at 10 percent of the lesser amount. It was at that point that I received a telephone call from Mrs. Zuski advising me that Tom had been arrested and that he wanted me to represent him. She requested that I go to the county jail, where he was being held without bail. When asked, she offered no other details about his arrest. When I got to the jail, I sat there in a conference room and listened to a story that I thought only Hannibal Lecter could think of. It seemed that for the past three years, Mrs. Zuski had been passed over for promotion, and she also felt that she was getting the worst assignments. She was certain that this was all due to her supervisor, whom she believed was prejudiced against her because of her ethnic background. She had become so obsessed with the conduct of the supervisor that she filed a complaint, which was rejected. Her conduct at home was so affected by this situation that she was driving Tom to drink, as the saying goes. Tom couldn't take it anymore, so unbeknownst to his wife, he drew upon skills he had learned in the underground during World War II and constructed a bomb with a timing device, along with a homemade version of a claymore mine. For the benefit of my nonmilitary readers, this is known in the Army as an anti-personnel device. It is arc-shaped and contains many pieces of shrapnel. Set on the ground, it stands only about four to five inches tall and is set off by a remote battery connected to wires long enough to keep the detonator far enough away to prevent the person operating it from being blown up. The arc shape allows it to be placed so you can aim the shrapnel toward the direction you expect the target to come from.

Tom placed the bomb under the supervisor's car and the claymore mine across the street from his house. The bomb went off, but the explosive was insufficient to penetrate the interior of the car. Dazed, the supervisor did not get out of the car. In a panic and worried about being seen, Tom ran from the scene, leaving the mine in place, undetonated. He was spotted by a passerby getting into his car, and it didn't take long for him to be arrested. Tom was a highly intelligent man, despite this act of madness. He reasoned that part of the lawsuit involving the car accident would include a claim of anxiety and depression. He knew that his only defense to the criminal charges would include an insanity defense. Therefore, he concluded, it would be best to have me represent him on both, so that the medical issues raised in both would not conflict. This reasoning demonstrated a highly sophisticated thought process, which was impressive. I told him that the only problem was that the criminal charges required an experienced criminal defense lawyer. He agreed to have me bring in a close friend of mine, Ralph, with whom I had attended law school and who would work closely with me. Tom agreed, Ralph was brought to the jail, and a retainer was agreed upon. After a telephone call to his wife, she delivered a hefty check to my office to cover our services, and another to set up an escrow for expenses to include, in part, our bringing in a forensic psychiatrist to examine him. We also requested that the court appoint a psychiatrist to conduct an independent evaluation of Tom. It was at that point that the roof fell in.

I received a letter and a call from a well-known criminal attorney that he had been asked to take over the case. Also, a letter came in from another attorney I knew very well who had been retained to take over the civil case. Finally, I received a letter from the Ethics Committee, along with a copy of a letter from Mrs. Zuski that she had sent to the Ethics Committee, claiming that her husband had been taken advantage of by Ralph and me. This was the first ethics complaint that was ever filed against me. When I called my friend, he immediately apologized, indicating that an attorney from his office had handled the matter while he was away. We met and talked about what had occurred. He told me that all the attorney from his office had done was to tell Mrs. Zuski that she had the right to file a complaint, but he said his office had nothing to do with the complaint. He agreed that something sounded fishy and promised to follow up.

True to his word, within a week, he sent a letter to the Grievance Committee, countersigned by Mrs. Zuski, indicating that it was all a big misunderstanding and withdrawing the complaint. My friend then turned down the accident case and told her to find another attorney. I also called the criminal attorney who had been asked to take over the case. Apparently, Mrs. Zuski had told him that she had misunderstood her husband, that it was not me that he wanted to hire, and that I had refused to give her any money back.

When I explained everything to him, he also smelled a rat. We agreed that the best thing to do was for us to both meet Mr. Zuski at the mental health facility to which he had been moved for the psychiatric evaluation and find out exactly what was going on. When we did, we discovered that it was Mrs. Zuski who wanted the change of attorney because she wanted to be in control of the cases and, ultimately, any money that came from the negligence case. She had apparently threatened her husband that she would leave the country and abandon him if he did not do as he was told. Mrs. Zuski was waiting downstairs and admitted to the attorney, who had a private conference with her, that I never refused to return the money, just not all of it. The attorney, Ralph, and I agreed how much we had earned to date, how much we had spent on Tom's behalf, and how much we would return, which I can tell you was not much at all. The attorney agreed that one office should handle all of Tom's matters and decided to take on the civil case, agreeing to a very fair lien in my favor on the attorney's fees earned in that case. He also wrote a letter to the Grievance Committee, before whom he often appeared in the defense of attorneys, indicating that there was never a basis for any complaint and asking that it be discontinued and expunged from my file. This attorney later went on to hold public office, enjoying a distinguished career.

Apparently, once a client files a complaint, it doesn't matter whether they withdraw it. It will be investigated anyway. It took the Grievance Committee nearly a year to respond, dropping all charges but asking for an accounting regarding the money I earned for processing the no-fault claim, which Mrs. Zuski had included in her complaint. When I figured it all out, it came to about $27 per hour. After another two months I received the Grievance Committee's final letter, generally cautioning the Bar that "any such fee be commensurate with the services performed." No one knows what that means. Should an attorney send a letter seeking reimbursement for a $10 medication outlay and expect to be paid at an hourly rate for the letter to be drafted and sent? Of course not! No other statute, rule, or law has been passed on the subject, as far as I know. I can tell you that to this day, no attorney I know is clear as to what that means.

The new criminal attorney was able to work out a very satisfactory deal for Tom, who did not spend much time in jail. I understand that while he was in jail, his wife divorced him and left the country. About two years later, I received my share of the fee on the civil case, which was settled just before it was scheduled to go to trial. Sadly, my co-counsel, Ralph, had died of a heart attack by then. He had never married and was an only child, so I made a donation to our law school on his behalf. What I miss most of all about Ralph was that he played a mean jazz piano.

I Know a Foul Ball When I Smell One

The cases that perhaps garner the most amount of attention in New York City are those in which a shooting is involved. A shooting evokes emotion from the viewpoints of all concerned.

It was not any different when seventeen-year-old Manuel Cruz was shot one Thursday evening. He was sitting on the brick stoop of his home at the left end of an attached row of identical homes. An alleyway was to his left as he sat facing the street. As he listened to the music coming from the large portable radio to his right, he had no idea of the events that were unfolding further down toward the end of that alley. Running as fast as he could was a nineteen-year-old with a gun in his right hand, with several Housing Authority police in hot pursuit. He had reportedly just robbed a local bodega. Later, the police alleged that the teenager had shot at least once in their direction, and they had returned fire at least three times. As he ran past Manuel's location, three more shots rang out, two from the police and one more from the teenager, who swung around to his right to fire in the direction of the police in pursuit of him. One of those shots struck Manuel in the right arm, ripping into his brachial plexus, at the base of his neck, and causing a partial severance of the brachial artery. Such a wound is life-threatening, and the loss of blood can bring about death in a matter of minutes if not treated immediately. Two of the police officers immediately summoned one of their patrol cars, put Manuel into the patrol car, and rushed him to the hospital, not wanting to take any chances that an ambulance might take too long to respond. One of the officers placed direct pressure onto the wound to slow down the loss of blood, which was flowing as if from an open faucet. His action most likely saved Manuel's life.

When the police and Manuel arrived at the hospital, personnel from the emergency room were waiting, since a call had been made from the patrol car alerting them to the situation. Manuel was taken immediately to the emergency room, where additional steps were taken to prevent further blood loss, which was of critical concern. Blood infusion was started, and Manuel was prepared for surgery. While all of this was going on, a priest who was nearby in the emergency room was called in, and last rites were administered. Now under heavy sedation, Manuel was taken up to the operating room by elevator, and a team of surgeons undertook a lifesaving, almost three-hour surgery to repair the significant damage that this single .38-caliber bullet had done. I am happy to report that Manuel lived through the surgery, but despite intensive physical therapy, he was unable to regain full use of his right hand and arm. The psychological damage resulting from this near-death experience was also significant.

To preserve the right to sue a municipality, a Notice of Claim must be served within ninety days from the date of occurrence; then the summons and complaint must be served within one year and ninety days from the date of occurrence. Investigation of an occurrence involving the police is never easy, as records sometimes become unavailable and have even, in some cases, been tampered with or forged. The claim that the bullet that went through Manuel's arm was never recovered was suspicious from the start. Nor was the bullet that the police claim was the first shot fired ever recovered. In fact, despite the opinion of an expert we retained that it was a police bullet that went through Manuel's arm, the police department never conceded that to be true. The case moved forward based upon the theories of the use of excessive force and the failure to follow appropriate protocol by engaging in an exchange of gunfire in the presence of an innocent bystander. During the taking of depositions, the police officers each denied firing the shot that hit Manuel, and the department denied making any attempt to take a written statement from Manuel at any time while he was in the hospital and, for that matter, at any time when he did not have an attorney present.

I first met Manuel after he was released from the hospital about thirteen days after admission. I was immediately taken by Manuel, who was as handsome a young man as I had ever seen. Of Spanish-American descent, he had a light-skinned, olive complexion, and with his wavy long black hair, he easily could have been cast in the lead role of a movie or Broadway show. During jury selection, lawyers often remind prospective jurors that clients and witnesses do not come from central casting. Manuel was an exception. While selecting a jury, I took the unusual step of having him sit at counsel's table and noticed that the jury kept him in focus at all times. After jury selection was complete, I was somewhat shaken to learn the name of the trial judge assigned to the case. This judge seemed to be assigned as trial judge to a significant number of cases in which the municipality was the defendant. At that time, the municipality was insured by a particular insurance company, and the same judge was assigned to many of the cases involving its clients. A large number of those cases were successfully defended, which gave rise to the belief that the judge was not an impartial jurist.

This was a long-standing concern of local attorneys for plaintiffs. My motion to have the judge recuse himself was denied, as I expected. I felt that the jury would be sympathetic to my client. I simply had to keep myself in check, no matter what his rulings. Normally, I try to put my own client on as late in the plaintiff's case as I can, since he gets the opportunity to hear other witnesses' testimony. In this instance, I decided to put Manuel on first, since I thought that the jury was going to like him, and he also was a very credible witness. His testimony was as good as I have ever elicited from a client. His testimony about being scared of dying when he saw the blood flowing, his pain as they put him in the police car, the pain as the car seemed to hit every pothole the city streets had to offer, and his experience in the emergency room where everyone was rushing to get him to surgery so they didn't lose him was compelling. Almost all of the jurors had tears in their eyes when he described what went through his mind as the priest gave him the last rites. It was at that point that the judge called me up to the bench and warned me not to intentionally "play upon the sympathy of the jury." All jurors, as part of their oath, agree not to let sympathy affect their verdict. They are not required to check their past experience at the courtroom door. I also remind the reader that the defendant's lawyer who participated in the jury selection had agreed that the jury selected was satisfactory to him. Why he allowed as many older women onto the jury was a mystery to me, but I assumed that he didn't think these jurors would be overly generous when it came to awarding money damages. After describing his feeling of nausea and drowsiness from the presurgical narcotics that had been administered, Manuel then described seeing men and women in gowns, wearing masks on their faces. As the operating room and everyone in it faded from view, he stated, with tears in his eyes, that when he remembered the last rites administered by the priest, "I thought that I had died and was now in heaven." Uniformly, all the jurors were sobbing when the judge slammed his gavel and announced that he was declaring a mistrial.

It took two years for the case came up for trial again. The delay was caused by the insurance carrier going into receivership, a special type of bankruptcy, freezing all pending claims.

Finally, the case was tried again. During that retrial, the police department was caught in a major lie when its attorney tried to introduce into evidence a statement the police claimed was taken from Manuel while he was in the elevator being taken to the operating room. Considering the department's prior denial that any statement was in its possession and that police never tried to take a statement, together with Manuel's sedated condition, the jurors got so mad that it took them all of seventeen minutes to come back with a verdict. As a general rule, a quick verdict is usually a defendant's verdict. In this case, the jury didn't need long to figure out how many zeros they needed to use to formulate the number to give Manuel the substantial compensation he deserved. I never had to try a case again before the original judge, since he refused to preside at any trial I in which I was involved. Not my loss, I can assure you.

Learning to Face Life

Everything about this particular trial was a learning experience. It was one of my first dental malpractice defense cases. It was one of my first trials that was held in the United States District Court, of which there are two located in New York City: one in Manhattan and the other in Brooklyn. The federal District Court judge was the chief judge of that district, and this was the first time I appeared before him at a trial. The other attorneys, particularly the plaintiff's attorney, were some of the best in the business. There were four defense attorneys; all veterans at the time except for your humble author, who felt like a fish out of water.

As the trial went along, the case turned out to present unique legal issues, which are always a challenge, not only to the attorneys but also to the trial judge, who may wind up making rulings never made before.

The case was brought by a woman who was married to a dentist in training. When the surgery that was the focal point of the alleged malpractice occurred, he was a resident, training in the area of maxillofacial surgery. The plaintiff, Mrs. Mary Jergen, was a woman in her mid-twenties, who, as she grew and physically matured, developed a facial profile marked by a lower jaw that was significantly set back compared to her upper jaw. Her husband, co-plaintiff Dr. Jergen, was a strikingly handsome man, muscular in appearance, with a light complexion and reddish hair. He easily could have been a poster boy for his profession. A decision was made by both of them that extensive maxillofacial surgery be undertaken to correct her overbite, to bring her chin bone forward, and to cause a major change to her appearance. Extensive preparation was conducted, with the joint collaboration of several specialists needed to carry out the plan, including a maxillofacial surgeon, a plastic surgeon, an orthopedist, and a dentist. A joint decision was also made about which hospital to choose for the surgical procedure. In addition to planning out the steps to be taken, sketches and ultimately a painting and facial model were created to satisfy the plaintiff that her new appearance would be to her satisfaction. In addition, and vital to preparing for this procedure, the plaintiffs were required to consult with a psychiatrist who, after an extensive interview, had to render an opinion that the principal plaintiff, Mary Jergen, was a candidate for this type of an extensive change of appearance. Without this opinion, the surgery could not go forward. A psychiatrist did give his approval, although concern was expressed that Mary's desire to undergo the surgery was motivated by her concern that as her handsome husband progressed in his practice, she would lose him to a woman as attractive as he was. It was also learned that she had financially contributed significantly to his schooling, a factor that she sometimes dwelled on.

Once Mary was satisfied that the outcome would result in the appearance she desired, final arrangements were made for the surgery to go ahead. At the couple's joint request, her husband, Dr. Jergen, was given permission to be in the operating room, since he was already a resident in maxillofacial surgery, although he was to have no hands-on participation in the surgery. The first stage of the surgery was to have the surgeon break apart her lower jaw. With the benefit of bone taken from her hip by the orthopedic surgeon, the lower jaw would be moved forward and the bone graft material would be used to fill in the gap. The dentist would wire the upper and lower jaw together, with the wiring to remain in place for six weeks, during which the patient would remain on a liquid diet. Next, the plastic surgeon, again with the benefit of graft material, would reconstruct her jaw and perform any other plastic surgery necessary to attain the overall planned result.

Simply put, not every surgery, no matter how competently and professionally planned and carried out, goes as expected. Without being able to explain at this late date and in medical terms the difficulty that arose, suffice to say that the contour of her lower jaw, when surgically exposed by cutting away the outer skin and flesh, simply did not allow for the lower jaw to be contoured as planned. When this was discovered during the course of the surgery, all present conferred. Dr. Jergen was allowed to sit in on the conference, and when a joint plan was arrived at, it was agreed that the alternate plan would not be put into motion unless Dr. Jergen agreed. Dr. Jergen did in fact agree to the alternate plan, which was sketched out by the plastic surgeon and shown to him. The surgery then went on to completion. Mary's face was dressed with gauze to prevent infection, and she remained in the hospital for about a week until she was discharged for follow-up with her physicians and dentists. It was left to Dr. Jergen, at his request, when he felt it was appropriate, to discuss what had occurred during the surgery and to show his wife the sketch.

Eventually, when Mary learned about the events in the operating room and saw what her face looked like, she became so distraught that she immediately sought psychiatric care and consulted an attorney, who commenced legal action against the four physicians involved in her treatment. After pretrial discovery, the case proceeded to trial. As the trial went on, it became apparent that there was very little to dispute when it came to the facts, particularly the events that took place in the operating room. Frankly, I did not consider the change in outcome to be significant. While there was a vast improvement in her appearance, Mary was never going to be mistaken for a runway model, and our expert believed that her stress was due more to her lack of self-confidence and her concern over her husband's future fidelity than her perceived appearance.

As the trial moved into the defendants' case, it also became apparent that my client, the dentist, had treated Mary in an appropriate manner and never should have been named as a defendant, nor should the orthopedic surgeon have been named. This seemingly complicated case really boiled down to three issues: Was the change to the initial plan necessary? What was the effect of the change? And most importantly, should the presence of her husband, Dr. Jergen, in the operating room, by operation of law, constitute a total defense to the case. In other words, by allowing Dr. Jergen to be in the operating room, did Mary impliedly designate him as her agent? If so, did his consent constitute her consent, thereby constituting a complete defense to the case? Before taking summations, the judge indicated his intent to rule in our favor on the issue of implied agency. Nonetheless, we summed up to the jury without informing the jurors of his intention, and the judge instructed the jury on the law that they were to apply in coming to a decision as if that issue was to be decided by the jury. The jury was then sent home and directed not to begin deliberation until their return the next day. Painfully aware of the effect that the judge's decision on agency would have upon the outcome of the case, the plaintiffs, Mary and her husband, finally folded under the pressure and accepted the judge's recommendation of a settlement, which was but a fraction of what they had hoped to recover. I am delighted to report that my client did not pay anything toward the settlement. The judge then did something that I have never seen done in court. On the next day, he did not tell the jury about the settlement and instead sent them out to deliberate. All the attorneys agreed to participate in this charade, which was brought on by the judge's intense curiosity about whether he was correct in his ruling on agency. He wanted to see how the jury was going to rule, even though the case was over. As it turned out, in disagreement as to whether Dr. Jergen was his wife's agent, the jury reached what was clearly a compromise verdict, awarding Mary a modest sum, less than the settlement, and awarding Dr. Jergen nothing on his derivative cause of action.

It is my understanding that the Jergens divorced about a year later. The terms of their divorce are under seal, which is standard practice in a matrimonial case. He remarried shortly thereafter. I am of course uncertain whether she ever got her money back that she paid for his education. I am happy to advise that I was lucky enough to marry the most beautiful woman I ever met. She has never asked me to undergo plastic surgery, although I am no Clark Gable.

Serving a Life Sentence

When selecting a jury, I will often ask a prospective juror whether a witness who gets on the stand and swears to tell the truth is correct in what he or she testifies. It is surprising to me how many prospective jurors answer yes to the question, stating that witnesses must be correct if they are telling the truth. It is only after I observe that a witness may be truthful, but wrong, that the prospective juror comprehends the difference. The time, circumstances, lighting conditions, and other factors are among the things a juror must consider in deciding whether witnesses, although believing their testimony to be true, are indeed correct. While the attorney selecting the jury does his best to wean out those who do not understand this concept, one can never be certain. What happens when a juror, naive enough to believe that everything he hears is true, gets to sit on a jury? Will justice still prevail?

Seeking answers to these and other questions about how a jury trial is held, I couldn't wait to get my first chance to observe my first big-time jury trial in person. I was still in law school and on midterm winter break when my dad, then a law assistant in the state Supreme Court, offered to get me in to see that trial. Although, with rare exception (and this case was not one of those), all jury trials are open to the public, this trial judge decided that he would bar anyone he wanted to from entering the courtroom. The judge I refer to was notorious for making up his own rules, regardless of whether or not they conformed to accepted practice. To further frustrate any member of the public from watching the trial, he also had large easel-boards strategically placed in the gallery to prevent a member of the public from being able to see the defendants, their attorneys, the witnesses, or the judge. Even by the end of the first year of law school, I knew that the judge's actions were contrary to the fundamental concept that the public is entitled to monitor how our courts are functioning and whether justice is being served. This judge had virtually created his own Star Chamber, a secret place where a secret trial takes place. He did offer a reason for his conduct. It was to protect the defendants from retribution, he announced, when questioned about his actions. He said he "was concerned that a policeman might try to kill one of the defendants."

You see, this was a famous trial that took place in the early 1960s concerning a tobacco store holdup. During the course of the holdup, two plainclothes detectives walked into the tobacco store, unaware that a robbery was in progress. One of the perpetrators opened fire, tragically killing the two detectives. Two defendants were later arrested and charged with being the two holdup men. A third defendant was later charged with buying the guns and being the getaway driver. All were charged with felony murder, a charge brought when the loss of life occurs during the commission of a felony, in this case the armed robbery of the tobacco store. Anyone involved in the crime, even the getaway driver, can be charged with felony murder and can be sentenced to death, which at that time was carried out by use of the electric chair.

I was one of two allowed to sit near the front side door to the courtroom, near one of the judge's staff members, affording me the unique opportunity to watch the faces not only of the witnesses and the judge but all three of their attorneys. The first part of the trial that I watched involved motions to prevent evidence from being introduced at trial, including an alleged statement made by one of the defendants to a friend. The trial took place after the famous Miranda case, which gave any defendant the right to be advised that he or she can have an attorney, does not have to talk to the police, and that anything said can and will be used against them in court. The friend allegedly told police that one of the alleged perpetrators had confessed to committing the crime. This "stoolie" claimed that he was held in custody in a room with several detectives for more than seventeen hours during which time he had no food or water, was beaten, and was burned several times with lit cigarettes. His statement contained the names of the three defendants and later became the subject of a landmark United States Supreme Court decision after it was allowed into evidence when the judge, after hearing the witness's claim of torture, asked the witness whether the alleged confession was nevertheless true. The high court upheld the conduct of the trial judge. Other than as claimed by this witness, neither of the two defendants charged with the holdup ever admitted to being at the scene of the shooting, nor did they make any other incriminating statements. That alleged confession severely damaged the defendants, since they lost their constitutional rights. Allowing this testimony into evidence violated the later enunciated "fruit of the poisonous tree" doctrine, which prevents evidence developed during an illegal search or derived from an improperly taken statement from being introduced into evidence.

I sat there astounded as the judge's antics continued, including his mastery of a technique known as the unwritten record: facial expressions, gestures, and whispers, all clearly seen and heard by the jurors, which never make it into the written record. Today, this has come to be known as body language. The judge's body language could not have been louder if he had used a bullhorn. And then there were his outbursts on several occasions during breaks when the defendants' attorneys were out of the room. The judge described one of the defendants as "Pig-face." Then, turning his attention to the other defendant, the judge blurted out, "You, with that narrow face and with those beady eyes, I'm going to see to it that you both 'go to the chair,' along with Pigface, if it's the last thing that I do." The judge acted as a cheerleader for the prosecution rather than as an impartial jurist, which was his job. On numerous occasions during a break, he would whisper to the court reporter, checking with him that certain of his intemperate comments were stricken from the record. This, of course, was improper and illegal conduct on the part of the judge, but the court reporters who worked in his courtroom were intimidated by him, and this was not a cure for what the jurors had heard.

To my mind, the high point of the trial came when the attorney for the alleged getaway driver, a brilliant criminal defense attorney who went on to become one of the best criminal defense attorneys in practice, had that defendant's brother-in-law on the stand. The attorney's goal was to counter prior testimony that came in during the prosecution's case. A gun dealer from Maryland had identified that defendant as having purchased one of the guns used during the shooting on a Saturday several months prior to the incident. The prosecution contended that this defendant then gave the gun to one of the shooters about one week before the holdup. The brother-in-law was an alibi witness who testified on direct examination that this defendant attended a party he gave at his home for forty people on the day the defendant allegedly purchased the gun. On cross-examination, the prosecutor made a fatal mistake of asking a question that he did not know the answer to. The prosecutor was trying to show that with so many people at the party and so much to do, the witness couldn't possibly remember everything that occurred at the party. Frustrated at his inability to break the witness, he asked the brother-in-law to tell the jury what, if anything, he remembered talking to about with the defendant. The prosecutor somehow was unaware that the brother-in-law was an attorney. Jumping upon the opening given him like a fox in pursuit of prey, the brother-in-law testified that "he and the defendant were discussing the parole the defendant was on and possibly amending its terms." The attorney jumped up and moved for a mistrial. He argued that this testimony violated his client's rights by bringing up his past record, clearly the rule unless the defendant elected to testify, which would open the door to his past criminal record.

The judge went ballistic, accusing the attorney of orchestrating this exchange of question-and-answer. The judge went so far as to say, "I invented that trick before you were born, and don't you think that you're going to get away with that bullsh— in my courtroom." He excused the jury, then carried on his rampage for ten minutes more, during which he threatened the attorney that he would hold him in contempt of court. He then adjourned the case for the balance of the day and bounded out of the courtroom like a wounded buffalo. The next morning, with no choice and not wanting to commit reversible error, he granted the mistrial, a major win for this defendant, whose only chance at avoiding the electric chair was to win a mistrial and get as far away from the tidal wave that was going to put the other defendants to death. How brilliant was his attorney? His client was found not guilty at his second trial, although he did go back to jail for two years for violation of parole, in this case for consorting with known felons, the two co-defendants, who had prior felony convictions.

As for the other defendants, neither took the stand in his own defense, and each was found guilty of felony murder and sentenced to die in the electric chair. Their automatic appeals were turned down, but months before the scheduled executions, Governor Nelson Rockefeller, believing that the felony murder rule was being misapplied by prosecutors, commuted their sentences to life in prison without the right of parole.

The "Pigface" defendant was transferred to the prison in Attica, where the famous prison riot took place several years later, and he later died there. The balance of this story shall deal with the beady-eyed defendant, who went on to gain notoriety that even the most skilled mystery writer could not have foreseen. To lay the groundwork for the balance of the story, I must go back to the end of the trial. Several times during the trial, I asked my dad, "How can he do that? He can't get away with that, can he?" As a budding lawyer, I was shocked at what I had seen from the judge.

"Shut up," was his answer. "He gets away with whatever he wants to, and if you ever want to be admitted to practice, keep your mouth shut and don't get on his bad side." And so I did what he said, not wanting my career to end before it started. But I could never let it go. As I developed as an attorney, I watched as another remarkable career also developed. You see, while in jail for life, beady-eyed and frail, this defendant enrolled into a number of educational programs available to inmates and became the first prisoner to be admitted to practice law in the federal courts. He specialized in matters concerning inmates' rights, as well as review of trial records, and several prominent federal jurists went on to comment upon his ability, opining that he was a better attorney than most who came before them in similar cases. He authored several books, and a biography about his life was made into a movie starring Tony Danza. Several times, well-supported applications for his release from jail were denied, opposed by police and other law enforcement groups who pledged to see to it that he served out his life sentence.

After I miraculously survived emergency surgery to repair three aortic aneurysms, I had a lot of time to think during several years of recovery, and I genuinely believed that my life had been spared for the purpose of doing good for people and revisiting any mistakes I had made during my life. Upon reading that this prisoner's wife and forty-six-year-old daughter, who had stood by him all those years, had both died within a year, leaving him abandoned and desolate in a prison located so far upstate that you had to fly there to make the round trip in one day, I decided that the time had come. We communicated by letter, during which I advised him that I was a law student who had watched his trial and wanted to meet him. He placed me on his visitors list as his attorney, and I met with him after he had served about forty-three years in prison. He was frail, confined to a wheelchair in the hospital wing of the prison, and dependent upon an oxygen tank to breathe. Although he was gravely ill, I don't think that he had been declared terminally ill when we met for the first time. We discussed the trial, his legal career, and his years in jail. He gave me a picture of his daughter, who had died six months before the visit, and we both remarked how much she looked like my older daughter.

We then concentrated upon the observations that I made at his trial and my strong belief that his appeals might have stood a better chance if I had come forward earlier. After all, he had never admitted to being guilty of his crime, nor was there any evidence, other than circumstantial evidence, introduced against him at the trial. We discussed the possibility of another appeal, based not only on what I could offer but upon his unparalleled record in prison and his rehabilitation, clearly evidenced by his legal career. At no time did he ever express any recrimination for my not coming forward earlier. If anyone knew how that judge could ruin someone's life, it was him. He said he wanted time to think about my suggestion. When I returned a month later, it was clear that his condition was deteriorating, and it was questionable whether he could live long enough to see through another trial and withstand the pressure. We also discussed how he would live if he were given his freedom. Given the go-ahead, I consulted with a nationally renowned appellate attorney, who agreed to handle the application for his release on condition that I furnish a statement and appear as a witness, which I agreed to do. I advised him that the appellate attorney was willing to handle his case, and he agreed to that attorney's fees, but his condition prevented him from going ahead with the application.

His life story was always the subject of conversation at the prison, heightened by my appearance on the scene. I got to speak to many of the prison staff, asking each how they would feel if he were allowed to go free. The opinions varied from "Yes, look how old he is. Look at his health and his legal career" to "Hell, no. The only way he gets out of here is in a body bag." My best estimate was that 60 percent were in favor of his release and 40 percent in favor of his dying in jail. I really believe that he and I could have collaborated and won his release. It just wasn't meant to be. He reportedly died of natural causes about a year later, although there are rumors. I dare not say more!

His experience convinces me that a new mechanism is needed to process the parole application of any defendant found guilty of bringing about the death of a police officer, since the present system is biased against a truly rehabilitated defendant.

Neither of us will ever know what would have happened if I had acted earlier. I do feel better having tried. I now devote a part of my time to coaching high school students who compete in moot court competitions, hoping to contribute to molding the character and skills of prospective lawyers. In doing so, I will be contributing to their skill and ability to fight injustice, no matter the cost. As for that prisoner, he holds the record in New York State of serving forty-six years before his death. His real name was Jerome Rosenberg.

Setting an Example

My wife and I were married a little over two years after we met. It was love at first sight, as she was absolutely beautiful. Since she never lies, I must accept that she too felt that it was love at first sight. It took two years for me to get up the courage to ask her to marry me, and we've been married for fifty-two years.

Our first daughter was born just about five days before I was released from active duty. Since my release was delayed about a week because of a paperwork snafu, that worked out great, since the Army picked up all the medical bills. As a struggling young couple with a child, money was tight so my wife pitched in and gave private piano lessons for almost ten years, during which time I worked my way up the legal ladder with three different firms, going from associate to partner in each. I must admit that as much as I tried, there wasn't time for much of a home life, although my wife and I have always striven to develop an interest in those activities that we each enjoyed. There simply was not enough time or money for me to have spent more quality time with our first daughter, who thankfully, as a working professional wife and mother, has come to understand, and we all enjoy a tight family bond.

Our second daughter was born about twelve years after our first daughter. I was by then a partner in one of the most successful law practices in the area. My wife and I had decided that the time was right to add to our family, so when we came back from a trip to San Francisco, my wife was with child. I promised myself that I would not miss out on the best part of fatherhood: quality time with my daughter. I also promised myself one more thing: I would never encourage her to become a lawyer. I just wanted her to be happy at whatever path she decided to follow.

When it came to including my daughter in leisure-time activity, I give myself a gold medal. There were horseback riding competitions, including ring jumping, hunter paces, three-day eventing, and foxhunting, which we both enjoyed. There was boating in our ocean racer and the smaller speedboat. There were ice-skating, skiing, rides on the motorcycle, and the auto-racing that she came to watch.

So on the first "Take Your Daughter to Work Day," I proudly brought my daughter to court with me so she could get a better idea how her father, who never had two dimes to rub together as a kid, could afford the comfortable standard of living that we enjoyed. I was on trial in Westchester County on a particularly difficult one-vehicle automobile accident case in which I represented the driver, who was the plaintiff. The claim was that there was a design defect in the roadway involved. The plaintiff's vehicle failed to negotiate a particularly sharp left turn, after which his vehicle hit the outside guard rail to the right, flipped over, went down the adjoining hillside, and came to a stop after hitting a tree. My client, John James, suffered a hip fracture and multiple right leg fractures, all of which left him with a severe limp when he walked, which he was able to do only with the benefit of a leg brace and cane. My adversary was an experienced litigation expert, a partner in a large firm that had years of experience in representing the county and defending it in roadway accident cases. During the pretrial discovery phase of the litigation, we had become friendly, and I learned that his wife was a well-known, respected horse trainer in the area. After the trial was over, she helped me find my first horse, which I owned for over twenty-five years until it died.

On the morning that I brought my daughter, who was then 11, to court, I introduced her to my adversary and to the judge after he took the bench. She sat behind me in the last row of the gallery on a wooden bench. While we were driving to the court, I explained as much as I could to her about court etiquette and about the case. Since we were still on the plaintiff's case, I explained to her about the witness I was intending to call that morning and the reason I was calling him. The witness was my roadway engineer, whom I was calling to testify about why, in his expert opinion, the design of the roadway was defective and, particularly, why the design did not comport with engineering standards. I had already put into evidence a number of accidents in that same location that were similar to my client's accident in order to demonstrate that the county was "on notice" of the defect in design, a key element in offering enough proof to convince the judge to allow the case to go to the jury. To prepare for this, it was necessary for me to educate myself on the subject of his testimony.

Not to pat myself on the back, but I must say that the expert's testimony went as well as I could wish for and, as experienced as Marty was, he didn't lay a glove on him during his thorough cross-examination. I was so engrossed in this phase of the case that it caught me entirely by surprise when the judge wiggled his finger, indicating that I should approach the bench. As I walked toward the bench, I noticed that he had a big smile on his face. When I got about two feet from the bench, he pointed to the rear of the courtroom. I turned around, only to see my daughter stretched out on the bench she had been sitting on when last I looked, fast asleep, with a gentle snore coming from her prone body. The judge's motion apparently also caught the attention of the jury, all of whom burst out laughing, as I did, along with the judge and everyone else in the courtroom. The judge then called a fifteen-minute adjournment to allow everyone to settle down and to give me sufficient time to go to the men's room and flush my face with enough water to regain my normal color from the deep red that I saw in the mirror. Needless to say, I woke my daughter up before leaving the courtroom. She was oblivious to all that had transpired, apparently having slept through all the laughter.

Unlike my older daughter, who announced when she was eight years old that when she grew up she wanted to be a veterinarian (a profession she now enjoys), my younger daughter took longer to decide what she wanted to do for a living, ultimately choosing to follow in my footsteps and become an attorney, much to my surprise. For the last fifteen years, I have been the proud father of an attorney as well as a veterinarian.

Oh, yes. John's case. That same afternoon, after digesting the expert's testimony, Marty made me an offer that my client and I could not refuse, and yes, that was the last time that my daughter agreed to come to court with me on father-daughter day.

Size Doesn't Matter

In New York State legal history, from 1920 to 2000, there have been a number of truly great litigators, giants in their field, be it criminal or civil litigation.

There are many who say that a great personal injury litigator can successfully litigate in any field because of the broad spectrum of issues that arise in personal injury litigation. Perhaps it is the ability to absorb the information necessary to present your case, cross-examine experts in a wide range of issues, and think on your feet that causes me to side with those who agree with this perspective. For example, to successfully cross-examine an expert medical witness, you must become as knowledgeable on the issues of medicine in dispute as the expert you are examining. It's not easy—I know, having been a successful litigator for thirty-five years, mainly in the personal injury field.

It is said that all it takes to start an argument is to put two lawyers in the same room together. With so many lawyers to choose from, I wonder whether those two lawyers could ever agree on the three "best of the best" trial lawyers. My three choices are made on the basis of having worked with them, against them, or having had the privilege of watching them in action. It's funny, though: all three of my "giant" picks were no more than four feet ten inches tall. This story will focus on one of the three, with whom I had the privilege of collaborating on a number of occasions and whom I humbly refer to as my mentor. For those he in turn loved and respected, he preferred that they address him as "Uncle," so I will do so out of my respect and admiration for his expertise and friendship.

An early 1970s study, published in the *University of Chicago Law Review*, found that 70 percent of all jurors had come to conclusions about a case after jury selection and opening statements by the lawyers. This conclusion flies directly in the face of the promises made by jurors during the selection process and the oath taken by them once the jury is selected. Before the trial begins, they must swear to keep an open mind and draw no conclusions until directed to do so and instructed on the law, referred to as the charge to the jury. The jury is then sent out to deliberate by the presiding judge.

"How could that be?" you probably will ask yourself. Are they all a bunch of liars? The simple answer is that until major changes were made to the jury selection process in order to save on costs, reduce court calendar backlogs, and increase efficiency, lawyers were allowed to take as much time as they needed to select a jury. Jury selection techniques were an art form, and no one was better at it than Uncle.

Why do I say that? How did he become so proficient at jury selection? In explaining the answer, it is necessary to talk about something that may sound very personal to Uncle, but I assure you that Uncle freely discussed what I am about to say. His wife, during their marriage, suffered from a number of emotional problems, which necessitated that she be under psychiatric care for most of her adult life and, on occasion, be institutionalized. Those who knew him well enough sometimes lovingly asked him if living with him may have been the root cause of her problems.

Yearning to better understand her problems, and to enable him to seek out the best care, Uncle read, studied, better yet *consumed*, everything available in writing within the field of psychiatry without actually going to medical school. He attended lectures, sometimes traveling worldwide to seminars to better his expertise.

His studies included pharmacology, and he also became a licensed hypnotist, since that was a discipline often used in treating his wife.

It should come as no surprise that Uncle quickly realized that his newly found expertise could be used in the practice of personal injury litigation, since it is not uncommon for a seriously injured person to develop an emotional injury. Uncle is credited with introducing psychiatry into the personal injury field and was often sought out to act as trial counsel for other attorneys wise enough to recognize the mental health issue in their case but lacking the skill or expertise to present the testimony in a court of law. Courtrooms were packed when the word got out that he was about to cross-examine a psychiatrist who sought to refute the claim of emotional sequelae, or aftereffects, experienced by a plaintiff. And so it was that as a young disciple of Uncle, already a partner of the firm I had clerked with for two years, I was authorized by my partners to ask Uncle to appear as our trial counsel in the case of Michelle Michaels, and to sit as second chair at the trial.

Michelle was seventeen years old at the time of her accident. She was a passenger in her nineteen-year-old boyfriend's car when it collided head-on with another vehicle.

Each driver blamed the other, which is great for the injured party, since state law provided that when two or more defendants are both responsible for an accident, the principal of joint and several liability applies. Translated into everyday English, the jury is then obliged to find the percentage that each is at fault, which must add up to 100 percent. The plaintiff is nonetheless entitled to collect the entire judgment from any responsible party if he or she so chooses. The percentages then apply when one of the responsible parties attempts to recover from the other the amount of money paid in excess of his or her percentage of responsibility.

Any competent attorney, including me, could have presented the liability phase of the case without difficulty. It was the injuries and the location of the trial, referred to as the venue, that presented the complexities of this case.

Michelle had sustained, among other injuries, very serious fractures of her left leg, known as compound comminuted fractures. Despite the best orthopedic care, she was destined to have pain, a marked limp, and gross, permanent disfigurement of the leg. For an athletic, seventeen-year-old, college-bound girl, these injuries were clearly going to affect her for the rest of her life. The emotional trauma she sustained later came to be known as post-traumatic stress disorder, a condition once associated with military personnel returning from the battlefield. It is defined as a severe anxiety disorder that can develop after exposure to any event which results in psychological trauma. This event may involve the threat of death to oneself or to someone else, or to one's own or someone else's physical, sexual, or psychological integrity, overwhelming the individual's psychological defenses.

Diagnostic symptoms include re-experiencing original trauma(s) by means of flashbacks or nightmares; avoidance of stimuli associated with the trauma; and increased arousal, such as difficulty falling or staying asleep, anger, and hypervigilance. Formal diagnostic criteria require that the symptoms last more than one month and cause significant impairment in social, occupational, or other important areas of functioning, such as problems with work and/or relationships. So there is no confusion as to whether this condition is real, lawyers cited a medical volume known as the Diagnostic and Statistical Manual of Mental Disorders, or DSM-III (currently revised and known as DSM-5), which is considered the bible in defining mental disorders. This treatise defines all known mental disorders and discusses each element of the disorder and those elements that must be necessary for a physician to make that diagnosis.

What complicates matters even further is that it is acknowledged throughout the profession of psychiatry that personal injury alone, absent direct injury to the brain, does not cause emotional injury. Rather, it is said that physical injury to the body triggers a pre-existing pathology, resulting in mental disorder. One exception may be in the case of a near-death experience, which can result in serious emotional sequelae absent any physical injury.

In order, therefore, to properly present Michelle's case, since she did not suffer an injury to her head, her attorney, Uncle, would have to dig deeply into her life to unearth any evidence that she was predisposed to suffer from an emotional condition set off by the accident and the physical injuries she suffered. Usually it's your adversary who seeks to bare the belly of the beast. In this instance, it was her own attorney who had to, with a deft hand, expose his own client's weaknesses in order to build the foundation of his client's claim of emotional trauma.

Wouldn't it be great if we could have a jury composed of twelve mental health specialists? Every attorney probably has a similar dream before waking up in a sweat in the middle of the night.

Unfortunately, that's not how juries are picked. The way it does work is that you are first assigned approximately twenty-four prospective jurors, selected at random by having their name pulled out of a large drum similar to a bingo drum. Once in a smaller selection room, the court clerk then picks out twelve of the twenty-four names, who are now the prospective jury, or panel. The lawyers, with plaintiff's lawyer going first, then begin to talk to the panel in the process known as *voir dire*. This is the only opportunity during a trial for the attorneys to speak directly with members of the jury. It is from these verbal exchanges that the attorneys are able to make their respective decisions about whether they believe that each juror can sit in judgment of the case fairly and impartially, as their oath requires.

So what happens if you look around at the twenty-four prospective jurors and they collectively make you sick to your stomach? Some attorneys will try their best to have one of the panel members say something in front of the others that is so prejudicial that he can then make an application to the judge in charge of all selections to disband the jury. Develop a reputation as an attorney who does that too often and it will get you in trouble.

Uncle, who I can tell you was no spring chicken when I met him, had his own unique technique. The judges all knew it was bogus, but given the deference paid to him, it worked every time. At the beginning of the selection process, Uncle would place into this vest pocket a currently dated medical certificate signed by his physician, stating that he was suffering from chest pains, that tests needed to be run, and that Uncle needed to be home on bed rest, ingesting plenty of fluids (most likely a scotch and soda). "Feel better," the judge would say, just before disbanding the "ugly" jury. It was amazing how quickly he would recover during the next day or two and be ready to go with a clean bill of health from his physician. What could the other attorneys do? Sometimes, you just have to grin and bear it!

Earlier, I mentioned that the venue of the case can be of extreme concern. Let's take New York City as an example. The Bronx is every plaintiff's lawyer's dream. Its population is dominated by minorities who, some lawyers believe, would "give the courthouse away" to a minority plaintiff. Manhattan is occupied mostly by renters, which means it is not the place a defendant wants to be if the accident involves a building defect. While these are generalizations, they often hold true.

It can generally be said that the county in which Michelle's case came to trial was not a good venue in which to allege and prove mental illness arising out of an accident which did not include a blow to the head. The population of the area was, to a great extent, Roman Catholic and Protestant, with just a small percentage of other religious denominations. Keeping in mind that this case was tried more than forty years ago, it was not an understatement to say that trying to teach psychiatry in this venue was like trying to teach atheism at a church service. To many in the area, psychiatry and voodoo were on a par with each other. Church doctrine often was in direct conflict with core principles of psychiatry. Also, the television was not cluttered with drug manufacturers selling the latest mind-bending drug, along with the warnings about the countless ways this new drug could kill you, as it is today.

Attorneys try their best to keep jurors off the panel whom they believe cannot be impartial or are likely to oppose their position, but each side gets only three peremptory challenges, which can be exercised at will or for any reason. Each side also has the ability to challenge for cause if the attorney can get the judge to agree that there is something about the juror that indicates the juror is not fair and impartial. A prospective juror may say that he or she is prejudiced and can't sit on this jury, in which case the attorneys usually agree to excuse the juror. It is an art developed by experience, the ability to convince a prospective juror to excuse himself or herself. Boy oh boy, does a licensed hypnotist have an advantage on that one.

And so it was at this time in history, in this venue, and with these issues at hand, that Uncle and I sat and watched as twenty-four potentially impartial jurors walked into our selection room, eagerly awaiting their turn to say, "I don't think I can sit as an impartial juror on this case," knowing that those were the magic words to get them off jury duty for the next two years. Since this was a civil trial, by New York law we needed to choose just six jurors instead of the twelve normally seated in a criminal trial.

After introducing himself, the plaintiff's lawyer introduces the other attorneys and the parties in order to determine whether any prospective juror knows anyone involved in the matter. If that proves to be the case, the person is excused on consent. Next, it is the plaintiff's lawyer's obligation to describe the case, cautioning the jury that the description is intended solely to determine whether there is anything about the case that a prospective juror should bring to the attention of the attorneys. If this is the case, they should do so, whether or not they believe it will have an adverse effect upon their sitting on the jury. It became immediately apparent that psychiatry was going to be an issue, although most of those who raised their hand on the first day were reluctant to reveal why they felt that they couldn't sit as a juror.

Since we didn't start until the afternoon, not much more was accomplished that day, which was a Friday. The weekend break apparently gave many of the prospective jurors the opportunity to think things over, because on Monday, one by one, either in front of the others or outside with the attorneys, the prospective jurors began to open up by explaining personal experiences with emotional anxiety, and experiences of family members and friends, seeking out advice from Uncle or showing their concern about whether these experiences would have an effect on their ability to serve. Uncle, with his kindly face; warm, soft voice; and years of experience might as well have brought a couch into the room, brought out a pendulum, and said to each juror, "Now, close your eyes," as he had clearly cast a spell over some of the jurors on Friday. Some had tears in their eyes as they looked at him, hoping that his words of wisdom would help resolve the issues they related.

Many of these troubled jurors wound up excusing themselves by uttering the magic words "I can't sit on the jury." It took the better part of three days for Uncle to turn the floor over to the defense counsel, who took about three hours to conduct the defense's *voir dire*, after which each side got to exercise its peremptory challenges. The six jurors we had picked were then removed from the room for the balance of the selection process, when alternate jurors were chosen, out of fear that something might be said that could affect their ability to sit on the panel.

Once all prospective jurors and alternate jurors are picked, the case then goes on a list of selected juries and awaits assignment to a trial judge. It was during this waiting period that Tom, the defense counsel who represented Michelle's boyfriend, came over to us and began to explore the possibility of settlement for the very first time. Until then, both defense attorneys had belittled the case, with Tom, who was himself a devout Roman Catholic, leading the charge. "Uncle," he said, "I've been giving this case a lot of thought, particularly after hearing your brilliant jury selection." He continued, "Trust me, Uncle, the trial of this case is only going to cause more grief to your client, so I've discussed the case with my fellow defense attorney, and we are willing to put together a settlement package of $125,000. I beg you, take it."

After thoughtfully considering the offer, but sensing that Tom was holding something back, Uncle looked him straight in the eye and said, instinctively, "Tom, there is something you're not telling me, and I need to know what it is before I can go back to my client and discuss your offer with him." By "my client," Uncle was referring to Michelle's father, Michael, who had been appointed as her guardian, inasmuch as she was institutionalized at the time of the trial and could not be brought to court to testify.

"OK, Uncle," Tom responded, "here it is. The real reason your client had a mental breakdown after the accident is that she and my client, before the accident, were having a sexual relationship. She was madly in love with him and a virgin when they met. About five months after the accident, he told her that he had met someone else and that he was breaking off the relationship. She began to cry hysterically, and that is the last time that they spoke. My client is intent upon taking the stand and telling this story. He feels he has to, since you also sued his father, who was the owner of the car, and he feels an obligation to protect him."

Consistent with the obligation of an attorney, we sought out Michael, who attended court every day. We went into a private consultation room, and Uncle, with heavy heart, relayed Tom's story and the offer of settlement.

At this point, it is imperative that you know a little about Michael. A devout Roman Catholic, Michael had been a sergeant of detectives with the police force for twenty-five years, and prior to that he was a military police officer while on active duty.

With a stone cold look of determination and resolve, Michael said to Uncle, "I want you to go back to the attorneys and tell them this." While finishing his thought, he reached inside his suit jacket and brought out a very large, intimidating gun. "You tell them that when Michelle's boyfriend gets on the stand and tells that story, I am going to take this gun out and shoot him right through the brain. And Uncle, when you tell them, make sure they know that I'm not kidding, so help me God."

I've never met anyone else who was as capable as Uncle of relaying that message. Clearly, Tom took it very seriously, because by the end of the day, the parties reached a settlement of $375,000, a significant sum in those days.

We all returned to court the following morning to advise the court of the settlement. The jury was put into the jury box, advised of the settlement, and the judge and lawyers all thanked them for their participation. Some of the jurors expressed deep concern for Michelle and expressed disappointment that the case was not going forward.

As if all that had transpired was not enough of a life experience, what happened next was even more surprising. Tom, this big, burly, devout Catholic came up to Uncle and sheepishly said, "Uncle, now that the case is over, I thought maybe I could get your ear for a few moments. I have an eleven-year-old daughter whom I've been having some problems with of late. Maybe you can give me advice on how to handle the situation."

The look on Uncle's face when he realized that the opposing counsel now accepted psychiatry as a viable treatment for his daughter's emotional problems was unforgettable. A month later, Michael resigned from the police force.

The Client Comes First

It is difficult to imagine being in a more precarious position than a personal injury attorney. Your retainer is contingent upon recovering money for your client. If you don't win, there is no fee to compensate you for your time and effort. You are allowed to advance disbursements on behalf of your client, but you are not allowed to offer to pay the client, no matter what. If you do, that is called champerty, and it is grounds for disbarment. At the end of a case which is lost, you have the obligation to try to recover your disbursements from your client, but you can't get blood from a stone. A change in the IRS code some years ago provided that you cannot even deduct the disbursements in the calendar year they are advanced. You are supposed to wait until the case is over and, even then, not until you have made a reasonable attempt to recover the money from your ex-client, even if it means suing the already unhappy former client.

When I was a sole practitioner, I estimate that at any given time I had outstanding advancements on ongoing cases totaling several hundreds of thousands of dollars. How can a new attorney open his own office as a sole practitioner in the personal injury field if he has not already hit the lottery or been born with the proverbial silver spoon? I have advanced as much as $80,000 in disbursements on a single case. Also, you are at the mercy of your clients, who have the right to change attorneys any time they want to. While you hope that your client will listen to your advice on whether or not to accept a settlement, you work for the client. The client is the boss, with the right to decline settlement or accept an amount of money you know is insufficient. And so it was when I decided to become my own boss as a sole practitioner; it all comes with the territory. Remember, too, your decision on whether to accept or reject a case is often dependent upon your prospective client's truthfulness. Perhaps there is no greater example than the case of Donnie Fazzio, whose story exemplifies the highs and lows of practicing law.

Donnie was a rebellious kid who lived in a neighborhood in which a boy was likely to wind up as either a criminal or a police officer. His parents' divorce did not help matters. His mom lived in the city, his dad in the suburbs, and he split time between each of them as he saw fit. At the age of nineteen, Donnie was on a trip to Florida with friends, hanging out, when a car in which he was a passenger was in a two-vehicle accident. As a result of the accident, he sustained several bad leg fractures. As luck would have it, the driver of the other car in the accident also was a New York resident, so after being retained, I was able to commence action against both drivers in New York. In addition to that action, I also represented Donnie in connection with a dispute which arose with the no-fault insurance carrier that was responsible for all of his medical expenses.

The issue that arose was whether he lived with his father or with his mother at the time of the accident. When the no-fault coverage of the car in which he was a passenger was exhausted, a claim for additional benefits was made to the insurance carrier that covered his dad's car. Assuming that Donnie lived with his father at the time of the accident, he would be considered an additional insured as a member of the household and entitled to the no-fault benefits provided by his dad's automobile insurance carrier. After the insurance company conducted an investigation, it refused to honor the claim, taking the position that he lived with his mom at the time of the accident and therefore was not a member of his father's household. His mother did not own a car, nor did Donnie, so no other insurance claim was available. The bills were substantial, so there was a lot of money at stake. The manner in which a dispute like this is resolved is referred to as arbitration, and it is held before a single arbitrator agreed upon by the parties. The arbitrator is usually a retired judge or an attorney. While it is to some extent informal, the arbitration is conducted like a trial: witnesses are called and most of the rules of evidence are applied, although the arbitrator has discretion to allow hearsay to come into evidence and give it the weight to which he deems it is entitled. The claimant has a right to an attorney (in this case, me) and the insurance company also is represented by an attorney. Although the insurance company is disclaiming coverage, the claimant has the burden of proof to substantiate his position by a fair preponderance of the evidence.

In this instance, it was a retired judge that served as the arbitrator, and given the amount of money involved, the insurance carrier had chosen a highly experienced trial attorney to represent it. The first two witnesses called were Donnie and his father, who both testified that Donnie had lived with his dad at his suburban home for almost a year before the accident, up to and including the day of the accident, as well as since the accident after his return to New York. Despite skillful and withering cross-examination, their testimony appeared to be sufficient to meet the burden of proof. This left the insurance company's attorney to put on its witness, who turned out to be the basis of its belief that Donnie did not live with his father at the time of the accident. Before I relate the testimony, I must take the liberty of assuring my readers that no disrespect is meant to the witness, or for that matter to the judge or my esteemed adversary, both of whom were Italian, as was the witness. It was simply the manner in which the witness spoke that made his testimony so memorable.

The attorney for the no-fault insurance carrier called to the stand a neighbor of Donnie's father who lived in a house directly across the street. The witness was a gentleman in his mid-sixties who moved to that house with his family about three years before the period in question. He was of medium build, grey-haired, and hunched over with severe arthritis from years of hard work as a laborer, both in the United States and in his native Sicily. He still spoke with a heavy Sicilian accent and to me was sometimes difficult to understand, although the judge, my adversary, and even my client and his dad had an easier time, since all were Italian and used to his manner of speech. Responding in as few words as possible to short, concise questions put to him on direct examination, he testified that during the year prior to the accident, he spent a great deal of time outside, often looking in the direction of the house across the street from him, and he never saw Donnie come or go from the house or the vicinity of the house. Satisfied with his testimony, the attorney announced that he had no further questions and turned the witness over to me for cross-examination.

After bidding the witness good morning, a habit of mine with all witnesses, I introduced myself as Donnie's attorney and told him I would be asking him some questions and to please answer yes or no, if possible, and not to answer my question unless he understood the question clearly, and if he didn't understand to tell me so that I could rephrase the question. He agreed, so I asked him to describe his home. It was then that he said that as a "city Italian," he was certain of his testimony. Although I had been brought up in a Jewish and Italian neighborhood, I had never heard the expression "city Italian" and was curious about what he meant. I will never forget his response. He explained: "Youa see, whena you livea ina the city, youra house no havea bigga property. Youra backayarda isa very tiny. So youa fixa up youra fronta yard with a nicea grass, a statue ora twoa, anda some nicea flowers. The fronta porcha is where you spenda mosta youra timea when youa are outaside, unda the awning, since it isa so beautiful." He then went on to explain that "suburban Italian" is different because the property is larger and the houses tend to have large backyards, sometimes with a pool. He then explained that suburban Italians do not usually sit on the front porch but usually spend their outdoor time in the backyard.

When asked, he said that Donnie's dad, Mr. Fazzio, "wasa suburban Italian becausa he had a beautiful backayard, a pool, anda he neva sata ina fronta his housa."

By this time, my adversary's face was bright red, as he tried to restrain himself from laughing, and the judge's face was contorted by his attempt to do the same. I then asked the witness if, when he sat on his front porch, the Fazzio house was directly across the street from his porch. When he said "yes," I asked the next question as fast as I could: "Well, if your porch is directly across the street, doesn't the house block your view of the Fazzios' backyard?"

He stopped for a few seconds, probably to think, since I was convinced that the witness was trying his best to tell the truth, and then said, "Yes, thatsa true."

I then asked him the $64,000 question (an expression that dates me back to the early Stone Age): "Isn't it also true that since their house is between your porch and their backyard, Donnie could have been in the pool all summer and barbecuing hamburgers without your seeing him?"

Again he paused, clearly searching for the truth. His response: "Youa know, youa right. Ia neva thoughta about it, but youa right. I'ma sorry, but youa right."

No longer able to restrain themselves, the judge, my adversary, and even the witness burst out laughing, as did my client and me. After a short recess to regain order in the court, the hearing judge declared that he did not require any more testimony and ruled in Donnie's favor from the bench. Any time I saw my adversary in court, we would both recount the story to anyone with us, and it never failed to cause us to laugh, as I hope you have in my retelling of the story.

All was not fun and laughter, however. About three months later, I received an urgent call from my client saying that he had to see me right away. I listened with outrage when he asked me what the outstanding settlement offer on his case was. When I told him, he instructed me to accept the offer, no matter what. At one point, he did ask if I could try to do better, but then he again told me to take what I could get. I pleaded with him not to accept the offer because I was sure we could recover at least three times the offer from a jury. "Why," I pleaded, "are you doing this?"

His answer was something that I will never forget. "I need the money to get a friend of mine out of jail. I have to post his bail right away," he explained. "He won't be able to take the pressure, sitting in jail. I have to get him before he spills the beans."

"Why you? That's his problem, not yours," I yelled.

"You don't understand," he said, "I was in it with him. If he spills the beans, I'm in deep trouble."

"For doing what?" I asked.

"You don't want to know," was his answer.

He was right. I didn't want to know, especially when the word gun crept into the conversation. As I mentioned, the client calls the shots, pardon the pun. So calls were made and the settlement offer was increased by $400,000. Once the case was settled, the bond was posted, and his friend was released— all within seventy-two hours, one of the conditions of the settlement. I must admit that I did make some of my losses back when I was retained to defend his friend on the criminal charges brought against him, but that's a story that we need not get into.

How, you might ask, is an attorney able to live with the uncertainty of what will happen to him the next day? My answer is: for the same reason that race-car drivers risk their lives, or scuba divers risk drowning, or pilots fly planes. Hey, wait a second; that's not an answer since I do all those things too. Hmm.

The Ruling Class

It was a veteran police officer who was the first to respond to the accident scene. Solely by chance, Officer Bob Green came by in his patrol car about three minutes after the collision that crushed Leon Wallace's legs. The officer later testified at the trial that the first thing he did after getting out of his cruiser and seeing Leon on the ground was to vomit all over himself.

The portion of the Belt Parkway that the plaintiff was attempting to enter, although well-maintained, had been constructed about fifty years prior to the accident and was, in many architectural respects, of poor design. For example, the entranceways onto the parkway were often located immediately after a stop sign and were extremely short before they merged into the right lane of the three lanes of moving traffic. In many areas, there were only two lanes for traffic, and often there was no shoulder on the right or on the left between the side of the left lane and the metal rail that served as the barrier between the opposing lanes of traffic. The court, during the trial, did not find it unfair for me to describe a motorist's attempt to enter the parkway at the scene of the accident as the equivalent of trying to win a zero-to-sixty speedway race, but with one of the two lanes ending, so that whoever gets there first lives.

Leon, alone in his twelve-year-old car, had come to the required stop before attempting to enter the westbound lanes of the parkway. It was his day off, and he intended to do some shopping in order to help out his wife, Marie, who was doing double shifts at the bakery shop where she worked as a salesperson. After stopping, when it was safe, Leon moved forward onto this twenty-foot entranceway, looking to his left by rotating his head about 115 degrees to his left. When he saw cars coming in the center and right westbound lanes, he brought his car to a stop to wait for a safe opportunity to enter the parkway. It was not unusual for there to be heavy traffic on this parkway, since the population in that area had multiplied since it was first constructed. After waiting about thirty seconds, he prepared to move forward by taking his foot off the brake, intending to move his foot to the gas pedal, when his car was hit in the rear by another car. As a result of the impact, Leon's car moved forward about ten feet before he was able to bring it to a stop by applying the brake. Leon sat there for about thirty seconds and collected himself before he opened his driver's door and got out of his car, which remained in the same spot where it had come to rest after the collision. His car was slightly left of center of the entranceway, but there were no shoulders on either side to allow him to reposition the car. Before getting out of his car, he did look into his rearview mirror and saw that the car that hit him was about ten feet directly behind him and also was also stopped. He also noticed that the driver had put the emergency flashers on, so his car was offered the safety benefit of that car's flashers, which could be easily seen by any other car trying to enter the parkway from behind the two cars. Although he turned off his engine, Leon left the keys in the ignition. There was enough room on the right, or passenger side, of each car for a third car to carefully get by on the right. This parkway permitted only passenger cars to enter, so truck traffic was not a concern.

Upon exiting his car, Leon walked to the rear of his car along the driver's side, and when he got there, he turned to his left to glance at the damage. There had been sufficient impact to damage the trunk of the car, pushing the trunk lid up enough that it was now misaligned, and Leon was uncertain whether it would close. He also noticed that his entire rear bumper had come loose and was lying in the roadway about four feet behind the rear of his car. Leon next turned his attention to the driver of the car that had collided with his car. Determining that she was unhurt, Jane Rose had exited her car and walked to the same area where Leon was standing. They greeted each other; she apologized; and then she walked to the passenger side of the vehicle, opened the front door of the current-model sedan she was driving, and got into the passenger seat. She then opened the glove compartment and took out the necessary paperwork, and there was an exchange of license, insurance, and ownership information typical in such unfortunate circumstances. During this exchange, Leon stood outside the passenger door of Jane's car while she sat in the passenger seat, having opened the passenger window, enabling them to speak and pass documents back and forth. While this exchange took place, both parties acknowledged that about ten cars had passed from behind on the passenger side of their cars and successfully entered the parkway. It is worth noting that while this exchange took place, Jane's emergency flashers remained on, offering both Leon and Jane the margin of safety that these lights are intended to supply.

It is only at this point that the stories of these two people began to differ. Leon said that when the exchange was over, he walked forward and was standing between the cars, facing the trunk of his car, with Jane's car still to his rear. He said he told her he was going to put the bumper into his trunk and then see what he could do about getting the trunk lid to close. He did put the bumper into the trunk, but after about two unsuccessful attempts at trying to slam the trunk lid closed, out of the corner of his right eye, he was surprised to see Jane's car go past him on his right, enter the parkway, and continue west until she went around a bend and out of view, leaving him exposed on the entranceway. Jane later claimed that when the exchange of information was over, Leon walked away from the window of her car, and she thought she was free to go.

Still standing out on the entranceway, Leon hastened to get the trunk lid down by slamming it with all his might. At that point, another car, the first to come along after Jane's car had left the scene, somehow failed to see him, striking Leon from the rear, then propelling him forward and crushing Leon's legs between the front of that driver's car and the rear of Leon's car. This was the scene that Officer Green came upon when he exited his vehicle and got sick to his stomach, sure that this man, who was screaming in pain and then went into shock, would wind up a double amputee, assuming he lived.

Officer Green immediately summoned an ambulance, and Leon was taken to a nearby city-run hospital, where he remained for almost eight months. Multiple surgeries were performed and although no amputation was carried out, Leon's left leg was left completely nonfunctional. He was able to put limited weight on his right leg and, with the benefit of crutches, was able to move from room to room in his apartment but was essentially rendered wheelchair-bound and in pain, dependent on medication for the rest of his life.

When Leon was first brought into the hospital, he was at best semi-conscious. It was about the time that his wife arrived at the hospital that a priest came into the emergency room, having heard of Leon's plight, and offered to perform the last rites. Mournfully, Leon's and Marie's eyes met, each, despite the tears, trying to look into the heart of the other. Having been married for fifteen years, it was no surprise that they both said yes to the priest at the same time. You see, Marie was Catholic, but Leon was Jewish. They usually agreed with each other, and both reasoned that Leon could use all the help he could get, either in this life or beyond.

In speaking to the nurses and other hospital staff during my trial preparation, I found them all to be uniform in saying that in all their years of service, they had never seen a patient in more pain for a more prolonged period of time than Leon.

That was part of the price paid when the decision was made, by both Leon and Marie, to try to save Leon's legs at all costs. Neither could accept the notion of amputation. That is why the head nurse decided that at all times during his hospital stay, Leon was to be kept in "bed number one." I learned for the first time that bed number one was the bed closest to the nurse's station, where they had the ability to monitor a patient twenty-four/seven and respond immediately to any problem that arose.

I also learned another technique used by the doctors and staff: the use of a placebo. Periodically, and without the patient's knowledge, instead of injecting the patient with a narcotic painkiller, such as morphine, the patient is injected with a benign liquid. This technique is used to make sure that pain medication is indeed still needed, to determine whether the dosage should be reduced, and to discover whether the patient is on the way to becoming addicted to the medication. Every time a placebo was injected, Leon's pain level increased, confirming that he was in significant pain throughout most of his hospital stay.

Long before Leon's accident, I had known that nurse notes were an invaluable source of information in preparing for trial. In reviewing these notes, I found a litany of anecdotal incidents which I felt should be brought to the attention of a jury once these records were received into evidence, occasionally with portions redacted. Never, however, have I had the misfortune of coming across an incident memorialized in a hospital record like the one I am about to relate. It is the custom and practice of hospitals to ask a patient if he cares to let the staff know of his religious background and whether the patient would like to be visited by a clergy member of his faith. By the time this incident occurred, it was well known in the hospital that Leon and his lovely and devoted wife, Marie, were of different religions. Leon had declined the request for spiritual counseling, although a social worker did regularly come in and offer counseling on secular matters.

No one knows then why the Orthodox rabbi entered Leon's room one day. Although the rabbi was uninvited, Leon, having been through so much turmoil, did not ask him to leave and, out of respect, welcomed him to sit down. The details of the entire conversation remain unknown. What was recorded by the nurse who happened to walk in and hear the rabbi's voice was the only portion of the conversation entered in her notes, together with Leon's immediate reaction. The rabbi offered the opinion that Leon's accident was payback by God for his having married out of his religion. Leon's scream was heard throughout the floor, and his marked depression after the encounter with the rabbi continued to be noted in the hospital record for weeks afterward. I am glad to report that the rabbi was never again allowed to set foot into that hospital. If you are also shocked, I am too. I am Jewish, and I have never been able to understand, forget, or forgive this comment.

A colleague suggested that Leon's attorney, Samuel Korn, consult with me about acting as Leon's trial attorney. It was an easy sell, as my reputation was now starting to precede me. After all, this looked as if it would be an easy case to try. The problem is, Samuel Korn had done his homework. He had found out that the driver of the car that crushed Leon's legs only has a minimum liability insurance policy of $10,000 in effect at the time of the accident. Imagine if that were all Leon could collect. I believe the expression in law is that it would be "compounding the felony."

Where else to look? Who else was responsible in law? What about a defective roadway case? Maybe, but by the time I got the case, it was too late to make that claim. The only other candidate was the driver who was no longer at the scene. It turned out that Jane Rose was the vice president of a large Texas company and was on company business at the time, therefore acting in the course of her employment. Even better, she was driving a rental car owned by one of the biggest car rental agents. Bingo! We found the deep pocket. Remember joint and several liability. All I would have to prove is that Jane was one percent at fault for the injuries sustained by Leon, and I could collect it all from the rental car policy, which was insured for millions. Certainly the car that crushed Leon's legs was mostly at fault, and without question, all defendants would claim that Leon was at fault for still being out on the entranceway to the Belt Parkway. If the injuries were not significant, it would not be worth the gamble, but given Leon's permanent injuries and permanent inability to work again, it sure was worth the gamble.

A significant amount of legal research and investigation went into my trial preparation before we were assigned to pick a jury. I was relying heavily upon a decision by the Court of Appeals (the highest appellate court in New York State) in which the plaintiff had pulled up to a metered parking spot to load luggage in his car in preparation to taking his daughter to college. While standing behind his trunk, the car parked behind him pulled out into traffic. Then, a car parked behind that one, while attempting to pull out, moved forward, crushing the plaintiff, resulting in the amputation of one of his broken legs. Although the case against both drivers was successful in the trial court, the Court of Appeals dismissed the case against the driver who was no longer at the scene, finding that there were intervening causes and that the first driver was not to be charged with foreseeing that the second driver would cause injury to plaintiff. Most unfortunate, since during the trial, the plaintiff, represented by one of the top trial lawyers, had turned down a $500,000 settlement offer. The jury had awarded twice that amount; now it was all gone. However, in what are known as *dicta*, which constitute language in the decision that is not considered to be part of the court's holding, one of the justices said, in words to this effect, that the ruling would have likely been different if the plaintiff were standing in a traveled portion of the roadway. A slim distinction, I know, but sometimes you have to go with whatever is available.

Jury selection was something else. There were three defense lawyers: one for the driver of the car that crushed Leon's legs, one for the rental car company, and one for Jane Rose and her employer. Each could not have been more different from the others. For the lawyer who represented the driver of the car that did the damage, this was what was known as a sit-in. He knew that his client was going to be found liable, but there was only a $10,000 policy, and his client was judgment-proof because he had limited assets. His participation in the trial was therefore minimal. The defendants' lawyers participate in the order that they are named in the lawsuit, so after the plaintiff, he went next and had little or nothing to say. Next came the lawyer for the rental car company. A consummate professional, Larry Dean was always brilliant in what he said. Part of that brilliance was in saying as little as he could. Every question was sharp and to the point. Every answer was calculated to be used in summation, and he never made the mistake of asking a question he did not know the answer to. The last lawyer, Tony DeRoma, was another story. Extremely successful as a defense lawyer, he was like a barker in a circus. Short and stubby, he often forgot to leave his cigar outside the jury selection room, and any question, no matter how outrageous, was never a surprise. For the benefit of those unfamiliar with court procedure, rarely is there a judge sitting in the jury selection room. The attorneys are expected to know proper procedure and decorum, and it is only when a problem arises that the attorneys adjourn the selection progress and go see a judge to seek a ruling on that issue. Having never picked a jury before with Mr. DeRoma, although I had heard stories, I never would have anticipated conduct like his. We made several trips to the judge and even had to have one entire juror panel excused because of prejudicial comments he made. After this case, anytime I had to lock horns with him again, I insisted, as is my right, to have a judge presiding at jury selection and even made history by having the judge grant my request that a court reporter take down the minutes of the selection process.

After twelve people and three alternates were selected for the jury, we were assigned to a relatively new but fair-minded judge with a reputation of letting the lawyers try their case, as opposed to a judge who constantly interferes with the flow of the evidence.

Every experienced attorney will tell his client to sit in a position as close to the jury as possible and where they see him as they walk into the jury room. I also gave Marie about $20 and told her to go out and buy the whitest athletic socks she could find, to make sure Leon was wearing a fresh pair every day, and asked that she raise the wheelchair legs to a high position so the jury could not help but see the condition that Leon had been left in for the rest of his life. One of the reasons for doing this was that the court had ruled that the case would be tried in a bifurcated manner, meaning that the first part of the trial would deal only with the issue of fault. Was one or more of the defendants responsible for the accident? If more than one defendant was responsible, the jury had the task of apportioning responsibility, along with deciding whether the plaintiff was also responsible and, if so, what was his or her percentage of responsibility. Only if one or more defendants were found responsible would there be a second half of the trial, dealing only with damages, when the jury would determine the sum of money that was fair and reasonable for plaintiff to receive. That sum would be reduced by the percentage of fault, if any, that the jury had found attributable to the plaintiff. So while the jury was not to allow sympathy to factor in when coming to a decision, bringing the jurors' attention to Leon's legs with the socks sticking out toward them, like a 3D animation, seemed fair to me.

On the third day of trial, the forwarding attorney, Samuel Korn, who was sitting in court every day, introduced me to his son, who was a second-year law student. One of the courses that he was then taking was Torts, and since this case was a classic tort action, he felt that his son could benefit by being there. There was a break at the school, and how better for a law student to spend his time? By approximately the fourth day of trial, it was apparent that the court was not impressed with my theory of the case against Jane Rose, and most of the rulings were going against me. My direct examination of witnesses was going well. Cross-examinations I found to be a learning experience. Usually, the attorney for the driver who struck Leon asked no questions. The examinations by Larry Dean were short, to the point, and after them, I always searched for the blood on my shirt, since the answers usually cut into my case. Then Tony DeRoma would get up, ask what he thought were a million good questions, and by the time he would sit down, you could see the rage in Larry Dean's face, knowing that all of his brief but brilliant work had been undone. By that time, I too had learned how to get under DeRoma's skin, how to light his fire by wording my objections in a sufficiently sarcastic tone. At one point in the afternoon of the fifth day, I had him so outraged that he got up and, in a bellowing manner, made about his fourth motion for a mistrial, accusing me of misconduct, which to this day I still do not understand. It was, however, at the end of this deluge, that he couldn't help adding, "…and in addition, Your Honor, you should declare a mistrial, if for no other reason than counsel's outrageous conduct in having the plaintiff wear those damn white socks every day." With that, he swung his bulging arm around and pointed his finger directly at Leon. I wish I had had a camera to show the face of everyone in the courtroom that day. You see, the money I gave Marie only bought so many socks, and with the pressure of the trial, she had forgotten to wash them. There sat Leon with black socks on his feet. Everyone in the courtroom, including the judge and the other attorneys, laughed hysterically—all but Tony, whose face was so red that the judge called a recess, fearing that Tony was going to burst a blood vessel.

I was clearly on a roll, so for my next witness, I called the defendant Jane Rose to the stand. This is a tactic that only an experienced attorney should use because the defendant is always going to be a hostile witness, but you try to use that hostility to your advantage. You must be careful, though. Never ask a question that you don't know the answer to; ask questions that call for a yes-or-no answer; and be ready to object if the witness is trying to sneak in something not responsive to your question. Based upon my discussions with the police officer, I knew that if I got the answers I wanted, this witness would provide testimony that would enable me to later demonstrate to the jury the key to solving this case.

As expected, Jane denied that she had seen the bumper in the roadway or Leon struggling with it as she departed the scene, leaving Leon exposed to traffic. The driver of the car that struck Leon also claimed that he didn't see the bumper in the roadway, which was not surprising, since he had somehow managed not to see Leon or his car. My next witness was the police officer.

After having him describe his initial arrival at the scene—how he became sick and then called for an ambulance—I went on to ask him about Leon's car, the damage, and its position on the roadway. I then asked him about the rear bumper, and he said that he remembered seeing the bumper in the trunk of the car. I then asked him if he found the keys to the car, and he testified that he found the keys hanging from the ignition, with the engine key still inserted, the engine off, and several other keys hanging on the same ring. When I asked the officer if he did anything to identify the other keys, all the attorneys got up and objected, questioning the relevancy. To this day, I do not know if they knew where I was going with this line of questioning. Fortunately, the judge overruled their objections, so I did not have to tip my hand. The officer testified that when he later gave the keys to Marie, he had asked about them and she had identified one of the keys as the trunk key. Later, in summation, every juror nodded in agreement when I asked, rhetorically, how the bumper could have gotten into the trunk if Leon didn't pick it up and put it there, as he had testified, followed by his attempts to slam the trunk closed. With the trunk key still hanging on the keyring and with the transmission key still in place, there simply was no other explanation.

With all of my success as the trial moved along, I still felt uneasy about the outcome. In his ongoing attempts at settlement, the judge continued to talk about the principle of intervening cause as applied to the case against Jane Rose. Could she foresee that the other car would come along? Was she liable after leaving the scene and, if so, for how long a period of time? I became more and more convinced that he was going to dismiss the case against Jane Rose. All this effort and only $10,000 to show for it! During the two-day recess declared by the judge, I probably slept a total of three hours.

When I arrived that next morning and saw the smile on Samuel Korn's face, I was perplexed. What was he so happy about? When he told me to "hold tight," my first thought was, "Hold on to what?" The court was called to order, but where was the jury? I was sure that when the judge took the bench, he was going to drop the ax on my case against Jane Rose. When he asked me to approach the bench, I did so on wobbly legs. He handed me a book and sternly said, "You have fifteen minutes to read this before we start." He then got up and left the courtroom. Several slips of paper stuck out of the pages of the book, a treatise known as the Second Restatement of Torts, written by the leading expert in the field, Professor William Prosser. In summary, the selected parts stood for the proposition that once you place a person in danger, you owe a continuing obligation to protect them in a reasonable manner. It seemed that the professor agreed with my theory of the case. Oh my God, the judge had bought into my theory of the case against Jane Rose! It was the way in which this epiphany had occurred that really knocked my socks off. It was only then that Samuel Korn saw fit to enlighten me. It seemed that the judge also had a son attending law school, the same law school attended by Samuel Korn's son. They were both in the same Torts class. The judge had become so troubled with the law of this case that he told his son about it and asked his son to discuss it with their professor. Seizing upon the opportunity, the professor set an entire day's agenda aside to discuss the case with the class and get their thoughts and input. It was only then that he wrote out his thoughts and gave it to the judge's son to transmit to the judge. That was the reason for the two-day break the judge had declared. It seems the law school professor's opinion of the law was identical to mine. We both were of the belief that having placed Leon in a position of danger on the road, an obligation arose to protect him from further danger. The class had ruled, and the judge agreed with the class; hence, Prosser's treatise on torts in my hand. Apparently, Samuel Korn's son was only able to talk to his dad the night before. That would have been a middle-of-the-night telephone call I wouldn't have minded.

You would think that everything would be smooth sailing from there. When the judge gave the jury the charge on the law before sending it out to deliberate, the portion of the charge on intervening cause was so confusing that Tony DeRoma asked for a mistrial by taking exception to the entire charge. Historically, trial practice dictates that an attorney only take exception to the portion of the charge he disagrees with. Not Tony's style. He always goes for the jugular. Doing what Tony did usually results in an attorney being held in contempt of court, but trying to keep his eye on the ball, the judge excused the jury, conferred with all attorneys, and composed a new section of the charge pertaining to intervening cause. Since I agreed that his first attempt was confusing, there was nothing I could do but agree. The problem was, the judge did some ad-libbing while re-charging the jury. I was afraid that an appellate court would reverse the decision on appeal.

While the jury went out to deliberate, settlement discussions were held. Finally, a settlement was reached for a substantial amount of money, with all parties contributing. What the judge never told us was that the jury had reached a verdict while these discussions were going on, sealed in an envelope. It was only after the settlement was put on the record that the envelope was opened. The jury has found Jane 10 percent at fault, the driver who hit Leon 80 percent at fault, and Leon 10 percent at fault for being out of his car too long.

Should I have let the case go to the jury and not settled? That is always the client's decision.

As for Leon and Marie, I am happy to report that I attended the wedding of their lovely daughter, Anna, presided over by Monsignor Tom Hartman and Rabbi Marc Gellman, who were famous for their TV program, "The God Squad." There wasn't a dry eye in the room as Leon, with the aid of his wife, then his daughter, a single crutch, and one morphine tablet, came down the aisle to give his daughter away. The wedding cake, three tiered and magnificent, was made in Marie's bakery—the one she bought with her share of the settlement funds.

There's a Stranger in Town

To be honest, we all harbor a little bit of prejudice. I'm not talking about racial, religious, or gender prejudice, although there is more than enough of those to go around. What I am talking about is a fear of the strange or unknown. When we travel to a different part of the country or enter a foreign port, sometimes we feel like a square peg in a round hole. Perhaps this is never truer than when an attorney travels to a jurisdiction he or she has never visited to represent a client at a trial. However, always ready for a challenge, I agreed to take on the case of Fred Stone, not only because of the challenges it presented but also because of the unique circumstances of the accident involved. To be honest, were it not for the fact that the injuries were fairly serious, I would not have agreed to be retained because of the expenses involved.

Fred lived on the southeast end of New York but decided to attend a state university as far north as you could go. He wanted to be a teacher, and by choosing a state school, SUNY-Plattsburgh, as a New York resident, he saved a great amount of money on his tuition. The drive time was about ten hours. The fastest flying route was to take a plane to Montreal and rent a car for a two-hour drive back to New York State and the college, which I did once when we were conducting depositions during the pretrial discovery process. It was also necessary for me to see the scene of the accident, since no attorney should ever handle an accident case without doing so.

As for the accident, it sounds like a scene that you might expect to be part of the famous movie, *Animal House*, about a college fraternity gone wild. In his senior year, Fred was the pledge master of one of the largest Greek fraternities on campus. Pledging was in progress on a cold winter night. There had already been a major snowstorm, and the temperature was near zero as a procession of four cars left the fraternity house that night. In each car, a fraternity brother was driving and another brother sat in the front passenger seat. Since he was the pledge master, Fred was in the passenger seat of the first car. In the rear of each car sat another fraternity brother, alongside a pledge, who was blindfolded to prevent him from seeing the route and, more importantly, where they were going to be dropped off. A prearranged route and destination had been chosen, located about fifteen miles from campus in a desolate part of the countryside. They followed an old logging road to the drop-off spot. It was a dangerous drive on a dirt road covered with ice and some fresh snow that was falling as they drove. About two miles from the drop-off site, there was a sharp curve to the right, which the first car, in which Fred sat, failed to negotiate. It slid on some ice, went off the road, and wound up in a snowbank on the left side of the road, alongside the middle of the turn.

Although shaken, no one was injured, and after a few seconds, Fred opened the passenger door with the intent of getting out and shining a lantern so the remaining three cars would be warned of their situation. Fred had one foot on the ground and was in the process of standing up when the second car approached, slid on the same icy spot, and also went off the road to the left. Unfortunately, that car did not stop. The driver, fighting to gain control and avoid hitting the first car, turned his wheel to the right and missed the rear of the first car, but his car went close enough to the passenger side of that car to hit Fred before hitting the inside of the open door, taking it off at the hinges.

Fred sustained fractures to both his right leg and right arm. About the only thing that went well that night was that the pledges were never dropped off, since they probably would still be out there, frozen to death, their bodies never to be found. They were all smart enough to realize that Fred needed to be taken to a hospital immediately. They drove him there since even if they had had a mobile phone, they never could have described their location to the police.

Fred did require surgery to repair the fractures of his right leg, resulting in surgical scarring. His right arm healed with the benefit of a cast. Although he was left with a slight limp and a small degree of limitation of function of his right forearm, the outcome could have been far worse, and these injuries were not likely to interfere with his desired career as a teacher.

About two months after the accident, I commenced a lawsuit against both drivers in the crash. Even my seasoned secretary laughed as I dictated the complaint, wondering how a jury composed of residents of the town where the college was located would react. Court rules required that I bring the action there. Although colleges usually bring money and business to a college town, prejudice can be a factor, and often there is no love lost between relatively affluent students and local townsfolk, who can be miles apart in their life experiences.

When I finally got word on a Friday that jury selection was going ahead on Monday, I packed up my midsize car with my clothes, files, law books, and even a typewriter and stationery in case last-minute papers had to be drawn. Fred had made arrangements through his old fraternity to have a student serving as a secretary on standby, in case I needed assistance. The Saturday drive was about ten hours for me, and even longer for Fred, who had graduated and moved back to the east end of Long Island after the accident. When I got there, it was minus 19 degrees, and that was before there ever was something called a windchill factor. Before I left, I went up into the attic of my house and selected two of the worst-looking polyester suits that I could find. The pants had cuffs and pleats. To me they were long out of style, but I was sure that they would fit in fine upstate, along with the three ties I selected that hadn't been worn in at least ten years. As the saying goes, clothes make the man. After spending all day Sunday in my motel room preparing (it was too cold to go outside anyway), I went to sleep early and got up early to meet Fred in the motel diner. I walked over and sat down after shaking hands. About three minutes later, a waitress in her mid-thirties came over and asked, "Coffee?"

I said, "Yes, please."

She came back about two minutes later and said, "Are you ready to order?" I said, "I'll have the number three, please."

I was so proud of myself, sitting there in my striped, polyester suit, blending into the local populace. Imagine my surprise when, ten minutes later, the waitress returned, put the food on the table, and then said, "May I ask you a question?"

"Yes, of course," I responded.

"Are you from England?" she asked.

In shock, before I could answer, I spilled my coffee all over the table, with some going on Fred, who was laughing hysterically, since I had told him of my plan to blend in.

Shaken, but not stirred, as James Bond would say, we finished this most unique breakfast and drove to court. Before jury selection started, we met with the judge, who was familiar with the case and managed not to laugh as I explained my position and made my money demand. I was then sent out of the judge's chambers; he conferred with my adversaries and then proceeded to tell me that they had no offer and were ready to begin jury selection. While both of my adversaries were experienced professionals, it was clear that they were playing good cop/bad cop, with the bad cop doing all he could to rattle me with statements like "There hasn't been a lawyer yet who came up from the city who was worth a damn."

At the beginning of jury selection, I made sure to advise the panel that I was from the New York City area and gained their assurance that they would not be affected by that or by Fred having been a student at the local college. Selection actually went pretty smoothly, all things considered. Actually, the entire trial went pretty smoothly. The local treating doctor was my only surprise because he agreed to testify for a fraction of the fee doctors in New York City charge for their court appearances. He explained that he had practiced in the city for ten years before moving up to the area, and he added, "I knew things would be different up here, given the local economy." Although I was delighted with his fee, his comment about "things being different here" was probably the last thing I wanted to hear.

About the only mistake I remember making was my failure to ask Fred to show the scar on his leg to the jury on direct examination. I remembered my error during the defense's cross-examination of Fred. When my adversaries finished, I got up and asked the judge to allow me to show the scar to the jury. When my adversaries both got up and opposed my application, the judge, after reminding me that Fred's direct examination was two hours long, denied my request. It was the only time during the trial that I thought I had gotten a hometown ruling.

Testimony ended late Friday morning. Since no plaintiff's attorney wants a rushed Friday afternoon verdict, fearing that a jury may find against you because they don't want to come back on Monday, I was happy when the judge announced that he would adjourn the trial to Monday for summations. Still, no further conference and no offer of settlement were forthcoming. Like a tiger in a cage, with the adrenaline flowing, I couldn't imagine spending a weekend in this frozen town with nothing to do. So I drove to the ferry, which at this time of year is a converted icebreaker, and took it across Lake Champlain to Burlington, Vermont. I was lucky enough to get the last seat on a plane to JFK Airport, where my wife was kind enough to pick me up. The next day, I learned that my older daughter was off from school on Monday. I was happy when she said yes to my suggestion that she return with me on Sunday and hear my summation on Monday since, unlike her sister, she had never been in court to see me work. The exciting prospect of a plane ride, the icebreaker ferry, and the trial were too much for her to pass up.

When we got to the courthouse on Monday, I was told by a staff member that the judge wanted to see me privately in his chambers. Upon request, I was allowed to bring my daughter to this conference. When I walked into his chambers, the judge stood up and offered me his hand. I introduced my daughter, explaining her presence. The judge then went on to say, "Well, Counselor, congratulations on settling your case. It's been a long time since I had one of you fellows come up here from the city who knew what he was doing."

I couldn't help asking, trying as hard as I could not to be a wise guy, "If you don't mind, Judge, how much did I settle for?"

He smiled and said, "Why, they have agreed to pay your demand."

"But, Judge," I said, "that demand was made before we selected a jury. There has been a week of trial since, and there were no further discussions during the trial. That may not be my demand now."

The judge walked out from behind his desk, put his arm around my shoulders and explained: "Son, I live about ten miles from the courthouse, on Route 83. My house is set back about 125 feet from the road. Do you know why I always back my car down my driveway in the winter?"

"No, I don't, Judge," I said.

"Well, it's simple," he went on. "At about 5:30 A.M., the snowplows come along, and they always plow me in, leaving a huge mound across my driveway.

The only way I'm going to get out to make it to court is to gun my car and shoot down the driveway with enough speed to plow through the snowbank they left across my driveway. So you see, son, jurors aren't that impressed with cars sliding in the snow around here. These attorneys like you. Tell you client to take the money and run."

It is my duty to tell my client about the offer and let him decide, so I went to Fred and told him exactly what the judge said, waiting for him to ask for my advice. Instead, Fred looked me in the eye and said, "Do you know what the difference between a driver from north of Albany is as opposed to a driver from south of Albany?"

"No," I answered. "Please, tell me."

"Well," Fred said, "when a driver north of Albany approaches an intersection and the light goes from green to amber, he hits the brake. When a driver from south of Albany sees that light turning, he hits the gas to make it through before the light turns red. I agree with the judge; let's take the money and run."

And so, my daughter never got to see my summation, although she did get a good lesson in life about how people can view the same facts differently. Interestingly, after the jury was told of the settlement and I got to talk to them, the first thing they asked was whether the scar on Fred's leg was really bad and whether that was why the opposing counsel didn't want them to see the scar. Truthfully, the scar was minor, and that's why I forgot to have Fred show it. It was a lesson for all the attorneys. Be careful when you try to keep something from the jury. Even when they're told to disregard something by the judge, it may only serve to heighten the jurors' interest.

The two defense attorneys took my daughter and me to lunch and fascinated her with their war stories, I assume trying to persuade her to become an attorney, like her dad. She still went on to become a veterinarian.

Timing Can Be Everything in Life

Having completed law school and then my six months of active duty with the National Guard at Fort Drum, in northern New York, as a mortarman, I started at my new legal position as an associate attorney with a law firm formed by the "Commish" and the "Judge," as they preferred to be called. Tradition has it that once a person holds a position of distinction, one is entitled to continue the use of the title and is referred to in written communication as Honorable John Doe, for instance. The Commish and the Judge followed that tradition.

It was not long before I was regularly in court, arguing motions and then trying cases. I must admit that I enjoyed the respect that came along with the territory of being associated with a firm that was considered by many, including sitting judges, as a highly respected firm with significant political clout.

The excitement only multiplied when along came Sergeant John Feeney, a member of the police force for twenty-five years. Sergeant Feeney was one of many police officers represented by the firm. During the Commish's tenure as deputy police commissioner of New York City, he had served as the police department's trial judge, presiding over departmental trials in instances where charges of wrongdoing were brought against an active police officer. If they were found guilty, officers could face anything from a slap on the wrist to discharge, which would result in the loss of all pension rights, if any had accrued.

Before the Commish held the trial judge position, many viewed that departmental tribunal as a kangaroo court that handed down rulings reflecting the will of the current police commissioner, whose decisions were often politically based. On the other hand, the Commish meted out justice as he saw fit and quickly turned the proceedings into a true court of justice. Within a short time, he earned the respect of the rank-and-file members of the department and continued to carry that respect long after he left the department. Our firm represented the NYPD Sergeants Benevolent Association, the Lieutenants Endowment Association, and the Captains Benevolent Association, as well as numerous individual police officers, both in connection with departmental hearings and on personal legal matters.

It therefore came as no surprise that Sergeant Feeney sought out the Commish to represent him at the departmental trial after he was charged with multiple (many hundreds) of counts of selling departmental records. If he was convicted at a departmental trial, he faced immediate dismissal, loss of his pension, and and an order for restitution of hundreds of thousands of dollars.

Hold on, now! Before you place him on the level of criminals like the Rosenbergs, let's take a hard look at this alleged wrongdoing. Within the police department, there was an office known as the BCI, or Bureau of Criminal Investigation. Sergeant Feeney was the head of this bureau. In those years, the late sixties, you could not just walk into a police station or courthouse and look up someone's criminal record, often referred to as a rap sheet. Unless you had a friend on the force, this type of information could not be accessed, no matter how legitimate the need, without jumping through hoops. Let's take the instance of an airline wanting to hire a prospective baggage handler. Before doing so, the airline wants to find out whether the job applicant has a criminal record and can't assume that he or she has been honest on their application. The airline then goes to a private detective agency to conduct a background search. The detective agency would then go to Sergeant Feeney and pay him $25 to get a copy of the applicant's rap sheet.

There it is—the whole ball of wax. Not exactly nuclear espionage. Mind you, I'm not trying to suggest that Sergeant Feeney was right in what he was accused of doing. I just want you to judge him based upon what he may have actually done and not upon the media spin, which made it sound as if he was selling investigative information concerning ongoing criminal matters. In his mind, his acts were so innocent that the document trail included checks used to pay for these records and, believe it or not, people even used credit cards. Cash was rarely used since these payments were written off as a legitimate tax expense by those paying the money.

After our initial interview, it was immediately apparent that Sergeant Feeney was in acute distress. In his early fifties, he was significantly overweight, suffered from hypertension and was diabetic. He seemed like a blown-up paper bag ready to explode.

The first thing we did was to have him fill out his retirement papers, which were filed the following day. Retirement takes effect exactly thirty days from the date of filing, after which his pension is protected, and the police department loses jurisdiction to proffer charges against him. Of paramount importance, his pension is then vested and can no longer be denied to him. Our next step was to take the accusatory document, which contained almost forty pages of single-spaced text itemizing hundreds of individual charges, and prepare written questions pertaining to each of the charges. This is called pretrial discovery, which can take many forms. The papers we prepared were a Demand for Bill of Particulars, Interrogatories, and a Demand for Discovery of Documents. It all totaled about 125 pages of discovery demands, and we were confident that the in-house police department legal staff would not be able to respond in the time permitted and would have to ask for more time. Everything we did was calculated to run the clock and get to the end of the thirty-day period without allowing the trial to take place, at which point victory would be ours.

We quickly discovered the lengths to which the department was willing to go when we learned, through inside sources, that personnel from multiple departments, including attorneys and secretarial staff, had been temporarily reassigned from other government agencies to aid in the preparation of the responses to our discovery demands. It was like fighting an army, as responses came pouring in without the anticipated request for more time. Something else needed to be done, and quickly. We put our heads together and came up with a plan. Matters were clearly taking a toll upon Sergeant Feeney's health. He looked haggard and depressed. He was not eating or sleeping, danger signs for a diabetic. We arranged to have him examined by a well-known internist, who urged that the sergeant be immediately hospitalized. The admitting diagnosis was depression, hypertension, acute diabetes, and male menopause.

We immediately made a motion in the state Supreme Court, by way of an Order to Show Cause, for an order staying the police department from going ahead with a departmental trial, on the grounds that the sergeant's mental state was such that he could not assist us in defending the charges against him, until such time as his physician found him able to do so. The court granted the interim stay and set a date for the oral argument on whether the stay should be vacated or continued. The argument date set by the court was on the nineteenth day following the filing of the retirement papers. Eleven more days and it would be all over but the shouting.

The next thing done by the police department was astounding. Instead of making a request to the state Supreme Court judge, which undoubtedly would have been granted, the police department took it upon itself to sneak a "police surgeon" into the hospital to examine Sergeant Feeney. So it is clear, don't be confused by the use of the term police surgeon. That is a generic term used to refer to any physician designated by the police department to examine and report about medical issues concerning any police officer. The physician who examined the sergeant, apparently in the rush to get him into the hospital to conduct the examination, was not properly briefed on why he was there, and he wound up sending a copy of his report directly to us as well as to the police department attorneys. As if heaven sent, his report agreed with the admitting diagnoses of depression and male menopause and also agreed that our client was unable to assist in his defense.

Upon receipt of the report I immediately went to the Commish and suggested that we hire armed guards, to be stationed around the clock at the hospital, with the intestinal fortitude to turn away any further attempt by the police department to sneak in another doctor. The next day, the police attempted exactly that and were, in fact, turned away by our troops.

All of this came out at the oral argument in the state Supreme Court, which was heated, to say the least. With the wisdom of Solomon, the judge kept things on track, ruling that the police be given another opportunity to examine the sergeant, after excoriating them for their self-help conduct. He held a follow-up hearing after the physical exam was conducted and a report was served upon us and the court. At that follow-up hearing, which was held on the twenty-seventh day, he vacated the stay and, after much conferencing, directed that the departmental hearing commence at noon on the thirtieth day.

The departmental hearing was to be conducted in the courtroom located at police headquarters, a stately-looking older concrete-and-stone building. The building had been the subject of terrorist bombing about two months before, and the entranceway was in shambles. In addition to armed guards at the entrance, there were security stations every thirty feet or so; everyone was escorted by two guards wherever they went, including the elevator ride to the third floor where the courtroom was located. Though we arrived on time, it was about 12:23 P.M. when the hearing judge took the stand and called the court to order.

The prosecution began its case and rushed through the proof it intended to introduce. It was apparent that they had decided to proceed with an abbreviated portion of their case, sufficient to bring about the sergeant's dismissal but keeping in mind that the clock was running on this, the thirtieth day. By the time they put in all their proof, it was about 4:30 P.M., and after a fifteen-minute break, the court invited us to start our defense.

We did notice that during the prosecution's case, a new court reporter was coming in and replacing the old one about every forty-five minutes. At this point, it is important that the rules of the road be explained. The trial judge, after listening to all the evidence in the case, is then required to make a written recommendation. That recommendation is then turned over to the police commissioner, together with the written trial transcript, to assist him in deciding whether to adopt the recommendation of the trial judge or to overrule him and make his own ruling. Smelling a rat, we made a strategic phone call during that fifteen-minute break (it always pays to have friends in high places), and we learned that the police commissioner was on vacation in the Bahamas, but before he left he had prepared his official ruling, confirming the assumed finding of the hearing judge that Sergeant Feeney be dismissed from the force for misconduct in the line of duty, and that he forfeit his pension. Unbelievable, you say. Well, if all had gone as planned, would the Commish have gone after this police commissioner and hearing judge for their wrongdoing, or were they gambling that politics would prevent him from doing so?

If there was ever any doubt, it was now crystal clear that we had to prolong the proceedings to midnight, when jurisdiction would end. So, we began by putting our first witness on the stand, the police surgeon who first examined the sergeant. Since we were armed with a mountain of medical textbooks, that examination started at about 4:50 P.M. and lasted to about 6:55 P.M. We then battled for and finally were granted an hour break for dinner. Once again, after advising the judge where we intended to eat, we had to go through security, in reverse, to get out of the building and walk to the Italian restaurant two blocks away. About forty-five minutes after arriving in the restaurant, four plain-clothes detectives arrived to speed us up and escort us back to police headquarters. It was while paying the check that I very quietly asked the Commish to hand me his reading glasses before he put them away. Thank goodness he didn't react when I slipped the glasses onto the floor and covered them with a napkin. I will always remember that smile when he realized what I was doing.

The process of escorting us back to police headquarters and once again going through security brought us back to the trial room by about 8:20 P.M. About ten more minutes passed before the court reporter took her seat, the hearing judge took the bench, and the witness took the stand. Opening the medical book to the correct page, the Commish reached into his pocket to retrieve his reading glasses to enable him to read a paragraph that would form the basis of his question. After bellowing an expression of dismay, the Commish advised the court that he had apparently left his glasses at the restaurant and could not proceed without them. Despite the judge's distress and obvious skepticism, he had a call put in to the restaurant. A search was conducted, and the glasses were found. Four detectives were dispatched, and the glasses were retrieved and turned over to the Commish. It was about 9:40 P.M. when the examination of the doctor resumed and about 11 P.M. when the Commish announced, "No more questions." The prosecution, of course, had no questions, as clearly, time was not on its side. The next witness was our doctor, who was still in the process of being cross-examined when the clock struck 11:59 P.M., at which time the hearing judge asked that all be seated and said: "It is now one minute before midnight, when this court will no longer have jurisdiction, and Sergeant Feeney's retirement from the police force will take effect. These proceedings are over. Good night, gentlemen." And he got up and left the courtroom.

The next day, in their afternoon editions, every local newspaper carried the story, blasting the police department, and especially the police commissioner, for bungling the case. The publicity for our firm was sensational. Our fee was huge, but the sergeant could easily afford it. Although he lived in a cold-water flat and drove a clunker of a car so as not to attract attention, I believe he had amassed a large enough bundle of money to buy a little island somewhere.

Not that he got to keep it all. It seems that the good sergeant did not pay taxes on his ill-gotten gains. The tax lien and penalties that we were able to negotiate, although considerable, still left him well-heeled.

We also represented him when criminal charges were brought, but we were able to plea-bargain a sentence of one year in jail. He served about eight-and-a-half months with time off for good behavior and an early holiday release. Of course, he was entitled to collect his pension every month for the rest of his life.

About two years after the aborted trial, a law was passed making these criminal history records accessible to anyone willing to pay the minimal fee to obtain them. Maybe the city should have sent Sergeant Feeney a thank-you card for showing them how to easily make extra money and how to make the city a safer place to live.

Tort Reform, aka Fool's Gold

At the forefront of the pressing question "Is today's government broken?" one of the talking points raised is whether we, the people, are in need of tort reform. Those in favor argue that reform is needed in the medical malpractice field, as well as in tort litigation, particularly product liability litigation. In a lockstep march in favor of tort reform are the medical profession, the drug manufacturers, defense lawyers, product manufacturing groups, and insurance carriers. At last count, lobbyists on their behalf spend approximately $4.5 billion each year on their quest for these reforms.

The sought-after reforms include, among other things: a cap on the recovery of money for pain and suffering, a cap on recovery for punitive damages, a cap on structured settlements, limits on the credentials needed to offer expert testimony, and limits on the imposition of litigation costs, particularly defense legal fees, upon unsuccessful plaintiffs. The argument is made that physicians are practicing defensive medicine to protect themselves from frivolous lawsuits and, as a result, the cost of medical care and treatment is significantly increased by the costs of needless tests. They also argue that too much of the premium dollar goes to defense costs rather than to the practice of medicine. They argue that premiums will go down if large awards are not paid to successful litigants.

The medical malpractice reform pundits fail to account for the additional costs of treating patients whose negligent treatment has brought about catastrophic injury or death.

It seems ironic that the political conservatives who argue that too much government has led to broken government seek to impose greater regulation on the practice of medicine when it comes to tort reform. Surprisingly, it is the liberals who argue for the status quo and take the position that the marketplace will provide any reforms that may be necessary.

It is often only when tort lawyers, at their own expense, demonstrate that a dangerous product has brought about serious injuries that manufacturers do a better job and produce a safer product.

The medical profession, pharmaceutical manufacturers, and their insurance companies run to the Congress with their highly paid lobbyists crying for help in the form of legislation reducing or even eliminating their responsibility and liability for negligence and carelessness. A prime example is the successful effort of gun manufacturers to be immunized against litigation arising out of their marketing practices. The tragic case of police officer Tommy Boone versus an American automobile manufacturer should help clarify the issues.

Prior to a fateful day in the late 1980s, after several years of award-winning military service, Tommy had followed in the footsteps of his father and grandfather and joined the police force. After several years, during which he earned commendation after commendation and high grades on promotional exams, his exemplary service resulted in his being named Lieutenant Tommy Boone. He was highly respected by his men, and there wasn't a police officer in the precinct who wasn't certain that Tommy's career was on the upswing. Although he had been brought up in a tough neighborhood where many of his contemporaries had turned to a life of crime, Tommy was a true role model, not only where he grew up but also in the neighborhood where he and his wife had moved after their marriage. Now a father of three, Tommy was involved in numerous local activities to help neighborhood children improve their chance of leading a productive life. Never forgetting his obligation to his own wife and children, Tommy interwove that obligation with community activities at the local YMCA, in Little League sports, and by introducing children to many cultural activities in order to broaden their perspective on career choices.

It was not surprising, then, that late on a Thursday afternoon, Tommy was sitting on the stoop of his attached brick home and babysitting his children, while his wife, Cathy, was at the local school, where she volunteered her time helping children in an art appreciation class. Tommy had ordered several pizzas for the family as well as for some of the neighbors. He made it a point to sit outside while waiting so he could keep an eye on the children who were out on the street playing stickball, a form of baseball played with a broomstick instead of a bat and a soft rubber ball called a Spaldeen instead of a baseball. In the back of Tommy's mind was his concern about the speed at which some of the pizza delivery cars were driven in the neighborhood. Fortunately, most of the local delivery drivers knew that when Tommy ordered the pizza he would be out there watching, so they minded their driving skills as they got to the block where he lived.

Sure enough, when the delivery car turned onto the block, the driver slowed down as he approached and then passed the kids, and he slowed down even more as he drove the last one hundred feet or so to where Tommy was sitting to the driver's left. The delivery car was an older Ford Pinto with the name of the pizza parlor stenciled on each side. The teenager put the gearstick into the park position and left the car running before getting out of the car, with the pizzas in hand, and kicking the driver's-side door closed with the back of his right foot.

As the driver took a few steps toward Tommy, the delivery car suddenly started to move backward on the street. Knowing that the children were still out in the street playing stickball, Tommy got up and ran as fast as he could toward the moving car, all the time yelling to warn the kids to get out of the way. Still athletic, he managed to get alongside the moving car, opened the driver's door, and was trying to slow or stop the car when he got caught between the inside of the open driver's door and a tree, ending up with multiple fractures and internal injuries. This was an accident that never should have occurred.

An ambulance was immediately called, and Tommy was put on life support and taken to the local trauma center. Since the incident involved a police officer, the street was cordoned off and treated as a crime scene. In addition to taking statements and photographs, the vehicle was impounded and thoroughly checked for mechanical defects. Police officers in New York City are deemed to be on duty at all times, and the police investigation confirmed that in trying to save the children, Tommy was in the process of taking police action when he was injured, so he was considered to have sustained injuries in the line of duty. This meant that his medical and hospital bills would be paid by the police department rather than by the no-fault liability insurance carrier that covered the vehicle involved.

Insurance policies do not limit the ability to sue for any amount. While a plaintiff does have the right to go after a defendant's assets, Tommy was not inclined to own a pizza parlor or the delivery vehicle.

Tommy sustained permanent back and leg injuries that prevented him from ever returning to work as a police officer. Although the police department did an about-face and tried to claim that his injuries were not disabling and that the accident did not involve a line-of-duty injury, I was successful in winning a Special Proceeding, brought in the state Supreme Court, which overruled the department, awarded Tommy his pension, and assured continued medical benefits for him, his wife, and their minor children.

Still, at forty-one years of age, Tommy had a reasonable work life expectancy of twenty-four years. Allowing for increases in pay over that time, Tommy, if he lived to sixty-five, was out of pocket almost $1.5 million. On top of that, Tommy had a reasonable life expectancy of thirty-five years, during which he would continue to experience pain and suffering that was reasonably expected to get worse as he grew older. In addition, Tommy's wife was damaged by Tommy's injuries by the many ways the injuries affected their relationship and enjoyment of living.

As I prepared to represent Tommy in a lawsuit, my search began for any third party whose actions, or lack of action, may have negligently contributed to Tommy's injury. The owner of the pizza parlor did his own mechanical work on the car, but the police department inspection found nothing of significance. Through an attorney who was one of the early internet experts, I was able to learn the mechanical history of certain components of this car, particularly the transmission.

Research revealed that as early as 1980, the National Highway Traffic Safety Administration (NHTSA) had determined that there was a defect in some of these transmissions. Refusing to acknowledge this defect, which permitted the transmission to slip from park into reverse, the company waged a determined battle to prevent disclosure of internal documents. These documents revealed that a recall would entail an expense far in excess of the costs of defending individual personal injury cases, including death actions, as well as any money the company might have to pay to compensate injured victims or the widows and children of those who were killed as a result of this product defect. The life and welfare of the public, including Tommy and his family, were reduced to a number on a balance sheet.

Armed with what I thought was a bulletproof case, I showed up for jury selection, only to find that this auto manufacturer would go to unbelievable lengths to either win the case or, if it did lose, to keep the verdict to a minimum. As I expected, the attorney for the car manufacturer was an experienced litigator who had defended many of these types of cases. What I did not expect was the attorney for the pizza company, who was one of the tragic victims of the morning sickness drug thalidomide, which led to birth defects in thousands of children of women who used it during pregnancy. He was born with no legs and with shrunken appendages for arms. He was able to walk with short prosthetics. Instead of hands, he had a hook at the end of each upper appendage. He neither sought not expected sympathy, and despite these disabilities, had managed to graduate from law school and earn admission to the Bar on his first try.

Though I respected him for what he had been able to accomplish, I wasn't sure how the jury would react as he sat there with a pen in his mouth taking notes. As injured as Tommy was, how was a juror going to ignore this attorney and determine the merits of Tommy's case and his case alone?

I telephoned the chief attorney for the insurance company representing the pizza parlor owner and suggested that this was an inappropriate choice of an attorney to try this case under these circumstances.

On the very next day, a new attorney appeared for the pizza parlor, and we commenced jury selection. The next time I saw the original attorney, he said, "No hard feelings. I didn't like the way I was being used." I went into the men's room and cried like a baby.

On the third day of trial, after the smoking gun—the car company's decision not to remedy the transmission defect—was entered into evidence, the case was settled. Unfortunately, I am not allowed to discuss the settlement under a confidentiality agreement. Disallowing confidentiality agreements would serve to protect the public by allowing for disclosure of manufacturing defects that cause injuries and even death. If you agree, please send a letter to your representative in Congress advocating for disallowing confidentiality agreements pertaining to manufacturing defects. Want to make any bets on who will oppose a change to this law disallowing these confidentiality agreements?

By the way, under proposed tort reform laws, there would be a cap on Tommy's recovery that would have severely reduced the money he received in the settlement of this case. Anybody want to change places with Tommy?

Two Strikes and You're Out

Don was the only son of neighbors, and he attended the same high school that both of my children attended. I have no complaints about the school, since both of my girls went on to enjoy professional careers. It was an above-average school district, with higher-than-average ratings for its wide variety of sports activities. As one rating said, the high school was a good bang for the buck, but not an academic wonderland.

It was ironic, then, that Don's nightmare of a day began during a gym period. At the time, the gym class, which was mandatory for graduation, was focusing on baseball. The spring season had just begun, affording the class the opportunity to attend gym class outside on the baseball field, something most of the kids, including Don, looked forward to. This was the first week of outdoor activity. On the Friday before, the teacher went over the rules of the game and the rules that the kids were generally expected to follow. These written rules had been prepared by the regular gym teacher who, about a month before, had become ill and was forced to take an extended leave of absence. In his place was a substitute teacher who had never taught a full semester and had never taught baseball as a gym teacher before. Despite his inexperience and the fact that "kids will be kids" to a substitute teacher, the students had actually been on pretty good behavior because the sub was a pretty easygoing guy. It was a beautiful day, so the class, after hurrying to change clothes in the locker room, formed up on the field that Monday in the early afternoon, ready to get in as much action as they could. Teams had been chosen the prior Friday, and a flip of the coin had settled which team would be up to bat first.

The sub arrived early, eager to get his first baseball game underway. Unfortunately, less than a minute after he got there, nature called for about the third time that day. Whether it was something he ate or simply a case of the nerves didn't matter; he simply had to get inside to the men's room as fast as he could, so he announced that he needed to go inside for about five minutes and left the student captains of each team in charge. Although the written rules reviewed on that past Friday indicated that the teacher had to be present at all times while a game was in progress, on that day the sub said nothing about what the class was to do in his absence.

Seconds after the door closed and the sub was out of sight, one of the captains yelled "Play ball!" and Don's team took the field. Don was assigned on Friday to play first base, a new position for him since he really liked to play in the outfield. After a few warm-up pitches, the first batter was up. "Ball one," yelled the catcher, who was expected, on his honor, to call them as he saw them. On the second pitch, the batter swung, and he hit a high pop-up fly ball that drifted into foul territory behind first base. Eager to make what would have been a difficult catch for even an experienced first baseman, Don, who was a good outfielder, kept his eyes on the ball as he chased it further into foul territory. A few more feet and he would probably have made a great play, but instead the ball just barely cleared the chain-link fence, which was about fifteen feet into foul territory. Concentrating on the ball, Don lost sight of the fence, which was a little less than six feet high. His face hit the vertical pipe supporting the top of the fence with enough force that he broke his nose; there were several lacerations, and it was estimated that he was unconscious for about twenty to thirty seconds. He was just about to get to his feet, with the help of two other boys, and was regaining his senses when the sub came upon the scene. Realizing what had occurred, and after checking out Don's condition, he assigned two of the boys to escort Don to the school nurse's office. He yelled at the kids, not only for starting the game but for also forgetting to assign a coach to take the coach's position near first base, in part to prevent such an occurrence by warning the fielder about the fence. (In this case, there was no dirt track along the fence, which warns a fielder that he is getting close to the fence.) He then ordered that play continue.

Don and his escorts made it to the nurse's office, stopping twice to give him a breather. After the nurse examined him and he yelled in pain when she tried to touch his nose, she knew Don needed to be taken to a hospital. She tried to call his mother but was unable to reach her at her daytime work number. She then called home and was able to reach Don's stepfather, to whom she explained the situation. He said he would get dressed and drive to the school as soon as he was able. It was not unusual for him to not be dressed for outdoor activities during the day, since he was a chronic heart patient who later underwent a heart transplant. The stepdad was told to look for Don on the sidewalk outside the main entrance to the school. The two boys were asked to escort Don to the meeting place. When they got outside and Don seemed OK, the boys, who were eager to get back to the baseball game, left him there to wait for his stepfather. He was sitting on the grass when they ran off. Unfortunately, the nurse never told them to stay with him while he waited.

As Don saw his stepfather's car arrive, he got up to walk toward the car, took two or three steps, got dizzy, and then fell backward, hitting his head on a rock. He was knocked unconscious, this time suffering a subdural hematoma with associated brain swelling. Meanwhile, his stepdad, having seen this occur, experienced heart palpitations. A passerby called an ambulance, which took Don and his stepdad to the local hospital trauma center. Don did not regain consciousness until reaching the emergency room at the hospital. His stepdad was also evaluated for his heart condition and did not leave the hospital until the following morning. A neurosurgeon was called in to evaluate Don, and the boy was taken to the operating room immediately to undergo brain surgery in order to prevent further brain damage secondary to swelling and bleeding within the skull cavity.

Before Don was discharged from the hospital about ten days later, his step-father, who was very active in the community and whom I had invited to be on the board of a local civic association when I had served as its president, contacted me. He also remembered me from the Boy Scouts case, during which I had received substantial press coverage and recognition. When I first heard about Don's experience, my immediate thought was to get my daughter out of that school, but my wife's cooler head prevailed. The lack of supervision by the gym teacher was inexcusable but at least understandable since he was a new teacher. On the other hand, the conduct of the nurse was about the worst case of nursing malpractice I had ever heard of. What was she thinking when she allowed Don to be unsupervised after he had suffered a head injury with a loss of consciousness, even for twenty seconds? Didn't the injury known as a concussion enter her mind? The school protocols she violated could fill a nursing book!

Following applicable law, I filed a Notice of Claim within ninety days of the occurrence, and a summons and complaint shortly thereafter. Not relying solely on the theory of lack of proper supervision with respect to the first accident, I hired a sports expert who went to bat for us, explaining why the layout of the field was improper and how these improprieties had contributed to the accident. First, the fence was too close to the playing field. Second, the lack of a dirt warning track at least eight feet wide along the fence did not afford the fielder the warning needed that he is getting dangerously close to the fence while concentrating on making a play. Third, the fence was too low and also lacked wrapped foam along the top pipe to prevent exactly what occurred when Don's nose hit the fence. The sub's failure to follow the school protocol and the nurse's malpractice were admitted to during pretrial depositions, almost causing me not to hire a nursing expert, but old habits are hard to break and I used the same expert that I used in the Boy Scout case.

The significant issue that required my attention was the lasting extent of the intellectual deficits that the brain injury caused and whether they were, to any extent, permanent. Again, a neuropsychologist was called in to evaluate Don's headaches, difficulty concentrating, and his short-term memory loss. Keep in mind that Don was a senior in high school at the time of the accident. Fortunately, he had filed for early admission to one college, using a relatively new procedure in which the student agrees to apply to no other college and also agrees to attend the chosen college, if accepted. Luckily, he was accepted, so the decline in his grades during the last semester did not affect his college acceptance.

But how was this going to affect his performance at this college, which was a highly rated university? Before leaving for college that September, Don was able to attend a number of remedial classes at a well-known rehabilitative center, making substantial improvement in his cognitive deficits; however, some degree of dysfunction remained, and what once was simple for him to retain now required greater time and effort.

Sometimes, you just have to be lucky. It can be as simple as being in the right place at the right time. On the day of jury selection, in came the same attorney who had defended the Boy Scouts case. Insurance carriers will put any attorney to the test if they even have a hunch that he is not ready or able to go to trial. He took one look at me, muttered something that sounded like, "Oh, s—," and asked me how much money I wanted to settle the case. When I told him, he asked me if I was sure that I had my client under control, because he didn't want to try to get me the money only to have my client change his mind. "You have my word," I said.

"OK, give me two days to see if I can get the money," he replied. After jury selection, only Don got to testify, and only in part. It was after the lunch recess that my adversary advised me that the money was on the table. As I drove home from court that day, I fantasized that, in baseball parlance, I was at bat and took a mighty swing, and I could hear the announcer yelling into the mike, "Holy cow, it's high and it's far, and it's over the fence, and it's outta here, into the parking lot, a grand slam."

It takes a lot of work to earn that kind of respect!

Uncontrollable Urge

One of the most iconic theaters in New York is the Washington Square Theatre in Greenwich Village, a unique venue where the audience sits on three sides of the stage, and one of the most acclaimed plays ever performed there was the award-winning *Man of La Mancha*.

I had the privilege of seeing this show with the original cast, featuring Richard Kiley as Don Quixote, when I was enrolled at New York University School of Law, which is also located in the Village. At the time, I was dating the woman who would eventually become my one and only wife. (It's now been fifty-two years.) She met me on a Friday evening, we picked up my car, and I started to drive to Washington Square when fate brought us past the Washington Square Theatre. Just then, a car pulled out from a parking spot directly in front of the theater. Ever the romantic, I pulled into the spot and said to her, "If there's a spot in front of the theater, there are tickets in there for us." Used to my sense of humor by then, she said, "Sure, and I'll wait here to hold the spot," which would have been interesting since she did not have a driver's license at the time. Keep in mind that this was the hottest ticket in town, even though it was an off-Broadway show at the time. As I approached the box office, I overheard the person in front of me explaining to the ticket vendor that a couple in their party would be unable to attend, so he was asking if he could hand the tickets back in. Need I say more? I paid face value for the two tickets, which were fourth row center. My wife-to-be refused to believe me until I showed her the tickets.

My next experience with a theater of that type was when I was consulted by Mrs. Marla Minion about her accident. Several weeks before coming to my office, she had gone to a similar theater to see her favorite heartthrob crooner.

As was always the case at the end of his show, the women in the audience were in a fervor and rushed down the aisles toward the stage, throwing flowers, room keys, undergarments, and anything else to gain his attention so he would acknowledge them by throwing a kiss or holding out his hand so that they could touch him. As luck would have it, Marla was sitting in an aisle seat in the ninth row and, as women came running down the aisle to her left, one of them, wearing spike heels, stepped on Marla's left foot as she lost her balance. The spike heel not only penetrated the flesh on the top of Marla's foot but fractured two bones in her foot. The pain was so severe that after the theater emptied, an ambulance was called, and she was removed on a stretcher and taken to a local hospital. Before leaving the theater, an incident report was created by the theater security staff. The identity of the woman whose shoe caused the injury was never ascertained.

Marla's injury was slow to heal, and although the broken bones eventually healed, Marla remained in pain, which not only intensified but began to migrate through her entire leg and into her back. After consulting several medical specialists, who attempted various modalities of treatment, the ultimate diagnosis was that, in addition to her foot injury, Marla had sustained an injury to her sympathetic nerve system, a condition then referred to in medicine as reflex sympathetic dystrophy.

I must confess that before dealing with this condition, I had never heard of it. Unfortunately for my clients, during the balance of my career, I represented four additional clients who also developed this condition after an orthopedic injury, and any physician who is educated in and has treated patients who develop this condition will tell you that there is no worse condition to treat, simply because there is no cure or antidote for the intractable pain suffered by the patient.

Originally labeled causalgia, this condition was first diagnosed during the Civil War and was associated with penetrating gunshot wounds to an extremity. The condition was unique and not fully understood because the pain could travel or migrate to other parts of the body, but not along known anatomical paths. For example, if the initial injury was to the left leg, pain could develop in the right leg, a phenomenon not understood by the conventional medical community.

There are several objective signs of this condition. The initial signs are increased nail and hair growth; severe burning, aching pain that increases with a touch or even a breeze; skin that changes in color and becomes dry or thin; and swelling or warmness. In the next stage, there can be a decrease in hair growth; spreading of the swelling; and stiffening of muscles and joints. X-rays will show demineralization of bone, along with muscle wasting. The pain can be so bad that an internal pump that delivers pain medications to the spinal cord is the only form of relief a physician can provide.

This condition, while not completely understood, is thought to result from damage to the nerves that control blood vessels and sweat glands. There is no known cure at this time, and unless it is caught early, it not reversible. Depression eventually affects most victims, and there is an almost 20 percent chance that the victim of this disease will contemplate suicide; tragically, some will go on to take their life.

Sadly, my studies also revealed the skepticism of the defense bar about this claim. I knew that I would be in for a battle when I decided to take this case. To prove liability was not going to be easy, since I decided that the only viable theory was going to be failure on the part of the theater to supply sufficient security to prevent an accident from happening during the stampede to get to the stage after the performance was over. I hired the best security expert I could find, and when I was satisfied that there was a failure on the part of the theater to develop a proper security policy, I commenced a lawsuit. After completion of pretrial discovery, I was by no means surprised to see Irving Gould, one of the leading defense counsels in the area, come into the jury selection room and introduce himself as the trial attorney assigned to present the defense. I was, in a way, happy to see him. First, I believe that I am always at my best when put to the test. Second, I always learn something from a skilled adversary. Third, seeing him there made me confident that the defendant was worried about a runaway verdict.

As anticipated, jury selection went along like a chess match between two skilled, evenly matched players. I could tell by the deliberate pace of his questioning that I was earning the respect of a highly skilled adversary, whose respect I cherished. It was about 4:30 in the afternoon when Irving asked for a short recess, during which he asked me if I would mind adjourning early for the day. I sensed from the look on his face that something was troubling him, but I didn't dare ask. He started talking anyway, explaining that he and his wife had a pet dog, Carrie, that was over sixteen years old and had been ailing for more than a month. Its condition had so deteriorated over the last several days that he and his wife had made a decision: they had to put the dog down. His wife had called over the lunch break to tell him that she had made the necessary arrangements with their vet. As he spoke I could see and hear each word get more difficult, so I begged him, "Irving, please, I don't need to hear any more; go home, do what you have to do, and send your wife my best wishes." Unfortunately, as a horse, dog, and cat owner, I could identify with his plight.

The next morning, I was ready to continue jury selection at 9:30 A.M. as was our jury pool. Irving did not arrive until about 9:45 A.M., unusual for an experienced trial attorney. You never want to keep a jury waiting and must be respectful of their time. He was about to say something to me when the jury clerk came in and told us that we had been assigned to a trial judge, who wanted to see us in his chambers. Usually, a trial judge is assigned after jury selection is complete, but sometimes if a judge is free, he may ask to see the lawyers when he is assigned the case and before selection is complete in order to acquaint himself with the case and see if a quick settlement can be reached.

We met in the judge's waiting room, and when he was ready, we were ushered into his chambers, introductions and acknowledgements were exchanged, and we were asked to take our seats along the outer edge of the judge's desk. In this instance, it was Judge Martin Monk Jr., whose father was also a judge for many years in the same courthouse before moving on to a distinguished career as an appellate court judge. He was a stately man who easily could have come from central casting, complete with a dark, three-piece suit, suspenders, a starched shirt, and a deep purple box tie, all topped off by a trimmed grey mustache and grey hair. Everything was neatly in place on his desk, and he and the room were the epitome of prim and proper. Having been in his courtroom before, I knew he ran his courtroom in the same manner.

Just as we were about to start talking about the case, his secretary advised him of an incoming call. As we started to get up to leave, the judge motioned us to remain seated and he turned his back to us, facing the window, so that his high-backed leather chair blocked our view, affording him the privacy he needed to carry on his telephone conversation. It was at this moment that I turned to Irving and asked him how his evening went. He said, "Well, when I got home, my wife was sitting there with Carrie on her lap, petting her. Carrie was staring back. I sat down on the couch next to them and before I realized it, my wife and I were crying like babies. It was as if we each read the other's mind; we decided to wait and stayed up all night." He then went on to say that early in the morning, when Carrie could not get up, they both realized that what they were doing was wrong. "I called our vet as early as I could; we took Carrie over at eight-fifteen this morning, and by eight-thirty it was over, she was put to sleep. My wife drove me to court, and here I am." As he was telling me the story, tears were coming down his cheeks and a shiver was going up my spine.

Just as Irving's story ended, the judge spun around to face us. His conversation was over. As his chair stopped and he hung up the phone, incredibly, he said: "Dog, did I hear someone say dog? Did you hear the one about the three dogs who are sitting in cages, side by side, in the vet's kennel?

"The first one says to the second dog, 'So, why are you here?'

"The second dog says, 'Well, I did it again. I don't know why I do it, but sometimes if I'm loose in the yard and the mailman comes, something comes over me. It's like an irresistible impulse. I ran up to him and bit him.'

"'So, what's going to happen?" asked dog number one.

"'Well, it's the third time, so they're going to put me to sleep,' woefully replied dog number two.

"'So, why are you here?' asked dog number two.

"Quivering, dog number one said, 'You know, it's the same thing with me, these irresistible impulses. I was lying there minding my own business. The paperboy comes along, and I swear that he must do it on purpose—he throws the damn paper and hits me with it right between the eyes. When I saw a certain look on his face that said *bull's-eye!*, I couldn't help myself; it was an irresistible impulse. I ran over there and bit him on the thigh.'

"'So, what is going to happen to you?' asked dog number two. "'Same thing,' said dog number one.

"'They then both turned to dog number three, who hadn't said a word up until then. They asked him why he was there. 'Well,' said dog number three, 'I also get irresistible impulses, let me tell you. My master is a handsome, smooth-talking bachelor. The women he brings home—one is more gorgeous than the last. Two nights ago, he brought home the most exquisite woman I have ever seen. I mean, they made love for at least a few hours. The next morning, he got up early and left her asleep. I pretended that I was still sleeping when she got up. Thank goodness the door to the bathroom was still open because I got to watch Venus take a shower. She was in the middle of drying off when she sat down on the toilet to relieve herself. That was it. I couldn't take it anymore. I jumped up and ran across the bedroom and into the bathroom. I mean, I made it look good, like I was sliding on the bathroom tile floor. As she got up, I slid into her, knocking her onto the floor, and let me tell you, for the next few minutes, I licked every drop of water from every nook and cranny on her body.'

"'Well,' cried out dogs number one and two, panting as they spoke in unison. 'I guess they'll be putting you to sleep, too?'

"'Hell no, she loved every minute of it!' exclaimed dog number three. 'Boys, I'm here for a shampoo and a haircut.'"

Having expertly told a pretty good joke, the judge was laughing hysterically, along with me and other people in the room. When we looked at Irving, he had both hands over his face; tears were pouring down his face profusely. To this day, I'm really not sure if he was laughing or crying as he excused himself, got up, and left the room, not returning for about fifteen minutes, during which time the judge asked me if Irving was all right. I never said a word about Irving's dog, and as far as I know, the judge never was told about the events of that morning which preceded the telling of his irresistible joke.

We then proceeded to tell the judge about the case. I sometimes believe he was happy that we didn't settle. Familiar with our abilities, he looked forward to an intriguing, different type of case and, like gladiators, we went off to the hand-to-hand combat of a trial. You could tell that we both had the attention of the jurors as we delivered our opening statements. The position of the jurors in their seats, their body language as each witness testified, both on direct and cross-examination, indicated their interest in the case. After I, representing the plaintiff, rested my case, I held my breath as Irving made his mandatory motion to dismiss the case on the grounds that the plaintiff's attorney had failed to make a prima facie case. Translated to English, this meant that it was the defendant's position that giving the plaintiff the benefit of believing everything the plaintiff contended was true, as a matter of law, the plaintiff must lose. The judge has the choice of granting the motion, in which case the trial is over; denying the motion, in which case the defendant's witnesses are called, if he chooses to call witnesses (the defendant can also rest its case without calling witnesses, and the jury can still find in its favor); or reserving decision, meaning he can delay his decision until later in the case.

Sometimes, an experienced judge will reserve decision in order to use this uncertainty as a tool to forge a settlement. He also may let the case go to the jury to see what they do. If the jury finds for the defendant, his decision becomes moot, and he will not be reversed on appeal for deciding incorrectly in favor of the defendant, which would necessitate an entirely new trial. In our trial, he denied the motion to dismiss, leaving it to the jury to decide whether the security was adequate. Only when the judge's denial becomes part of the record can the plaintiff's attorney take a painless breath. It's like all the air is sucked out of the courtroom until you hear those words, "Motion denied."

It was the defendant's third witness who made this case stand out as unique. He was one of the security guards that night. He testified that he was seated near the stage at the bottom of the row to the left of the plaintiff and that at the end of the show, it was his job to stand up to wave off and discourage audience members from rushing the stage. On cross-examination, I had to ward off the damaging effect of this testimony. Until then, it had not come out that the husband of the couple that accompanied Marla to the theater that night had taken several photographs during the performance. They say a picture can speak a thousand words. One of the pictures clearly showed a guard, in uniform, with a beard identical to the witness's, seated not at the bottom of the aisle on the row where Marla was seated, as he testified, but rather at the bottom of the aisle one section to the left. When he was shown the picture, the witness gasped, studied the picture, identified himself, and began to weep. By the time he left the stand, everyone in the courtroom was convinced that the witness had been honestly mistaken and was genuinely sorry. The picture was accepted into evidence; the jury was excused for the weekend; and the defense rested. We met in chambers, and the judge conducted further settlement discussions, urging that his recommendation be given serious consideration by all parties. No trial, whether truth or fiction, could end on a more dramatic note. This was better than any on- or off-Broadway show. Or so everyone thought.

Nowadays, there are movies, particularly on television, that offer an alternative ending. Prerelease screenings often offer the audience a chance to provide input into how the final release will end. This trial foreshadowed that format. On Monday morning, before summations, I was met by Irving, who, in a breathless manner, advised me that he wanted to have a conference before the judge took the bench. If it were not Irving making this request, I would have thought it was a joke. Irving made an application to reopen the defense case and recall the security guard to the stand. Required to make what is known as an offer of proof, Irving went on to explain that the security guard, so upset at what had transpired, had searched his garage over the weekend. Through a series of photographs that he had brought to court, he was prepared to testify that the photographs refreshed his recollection that during the year of the accident, for about ten months, including the day of the accident, an infection caused by an ingrown hair had caused him to shave off his beard. One of the photographs showed him in a tuxedo, attending a wedding, and sure enough, there he was, dancing with his wife, cleanly shaven. Seeing was believing. The security guard had wrongly identified himself on the stand. Once again, a picture spoke a thousand words, but this time, the words were different. I must admit that after listening to this offer of proof from the witness, without the jury present, I was convinced that he was again being truthful, and this time correct.

It would have been interesting to see the faces of the jurors listening to this testimony, because clearly the defense was correct, and the judge would have granted the motion to reopen the defense's case. Fortunately, the weekend had a sobering effect upon the defendant, who was also convinced of the truthfulness of the plaintiff's doctors. The case was settled. By agreement, the amount of the settlement remains sealed, since the defense bar was still not ready to concede to the existence of reflex sympathetic dystrophy, a condition that is now recognized by the medical profession and referred to as complex regional pain syndrome, for which there still is no cure. The best treatment for temporary relief of the pain is conceded by many medical professionals to be acupuncture. Unfortunately, one of the reasons I consider myself to be an expert concerning this injury is that my wife has suffered from complex regional pain syndrome for over twenty years as a result of a life-threatening automobile accident.

United We Stand

This is not a story for the faint of heart. It is a story defining the joy and blessing that the family union contributes to the human experience. You will come to know and love each member of the Snyder family, especially Steve, whose life was so dramatically affected one summer day when he was tragically in the wrong place at the wrong time.

Maybe I should say that it was the defendant driver who was in the wrong place at the wrong time. The driver, Ed, worked for a lumber company located east of New York City. That morning, the company had many deliveries to make, so to handle them all, the owner asked his son, who also worked for the company, whether they could borrow a pickup truck owned by one of the son's friends. The friend was happy to help, so that morning, the friend's truck was loaded with many two-by-four lumber boards of varying lengths, between eight and twelve feet long. There were also various other construction materials on the truck, all to be delivered to a construction site located about twenty-five miles to the west of the lumberyard. The driver, Ed, set out to make the delivery, alone in the truck.

After driving several blocks on local streets, Ed made a right turn onto a roadway which had two lanes for traffic in each direction, separated only by a double yellow line. He had traveled about seven miles on that roadway when he received a call on the two-way radio, advising him that a variety of nails that were supposed to be included in the shipment had not been put on the truck, and once his location was determined, he was instructed to turn around and return to the lumberyard so the error could be corrected. Traffic was light in both directions, so he made a U-turn and headed back, this time traveling in an easterly direction on the same roadway.

At about the same time, at a point about a mile east of where Ed had made the right turn onto that roadway, Steve walked out of a Dunkin' Donuts, coffee in hand, and got into his SUV. He left the parking lot by making a right turn onto that same roadway, heading in a westerly direction. He finished his coffee while heading for one of his dad's businesses, a retail store where he worked as an assistant manager. He was about nineteen years old at the time, having the great fortune of having been adopted at birth by two wonderful people. His adoptive parents, after years during which they tried unsuccessfully to conceive children naturally, decided to adopt. Steve was the second child to be adopted, the first being his adopted sister, who was also adopted at birth and was two years older than Steve. As is often the case, though it's still not fully understood by the medical profession, about a year later, Steve's mom discovered that she was pregnant, and she went on to deliver a full-term baby girl. At the appropriate ages, all were told how the family had gotten together, and there was nothing but love and affection between all members of the family.

Back to the scene at hand. As the two cars, now on the same road but heading in opposite directions, came closer, Ed came upon a sharp turn to his right. He was traveling too fast, and as his truck was halfway through the turn, the lumber in the truck shifted, the ties holding them in place snapped, and a number of the boards came flying out of the bed of the truck. Without any warning, the only thing Steve had time to do was to apply the brakes, at which time one of the boards, as if it were a lance thrown by an ancient warrior, hit the front windshield, penetrated it, and struck the left side of Steve's forehead, smashing the left side of his skull before going halfway through the back window and coming to a stop, protruding through the back window as the SUV hit a light pole and stopped. The pickup truck traveled about another 250 feet before it came to a stop.

Numerous agencies responded to the scene, none of which had any record of who first called 9-1-1. A local newspaper ran a story about the accident, along with a picture of Steve's SUV. Another picture taken by a helicopter news crew also appeared in the newspaper. It was taken in the dark, long after the accident scene and details of the roadway could be made out. Ed, on advice of his boss, who was called to the scene by him on the two-way radio, refused to make any statement about the accident. Steve was unconscious at the scene, remained in a coma for more than two months, and has no recollection of the accident. Although there was enough brain damage to cause amnesia, doctors never can be sure whether the amnesia was caused by the brain damage or by the remarkable ability of the brain to block out events that would simply be too unpleasant and painful to remember. Anyone familiar with Steve's injuries considered it a miracle that he lived long enough to get to a hospital, where he remained for the better part of six months.

Following admission to the county hospital, emergency surgery was undertaken to repair the massive skull fractures and to address the brain injuries, swelling of the brain tissue, and bleeding. The skull had to remain open for the time necessary to prevent further damage from swelling or the accumulation of fluid. Intensive, round-the-clock nursing care was required. Fortunately, the physician responsible for developing a modality of care for coma patients was called in, having developed that care following years of study at that hospital. There are several levels of coma, starting at Level I, the mildest degree, up to Level VIII, the deepest degree of coma, on the scale formulated on the West Coast and known as the Rancho Los Amigos Levels of Cognitive Functioning, as discussed in an earlier chapter. The physician I refer to concluded after years of study that, depending on the level, a patient in a coma, no matter how prolonged, can actually hear the sound of the spoken word, retain those words, and relate them if the patient recovers from the coma and regains consciousness. Although his family realized that Steve was a Level VIII coma patient, his mom and dad, along with his two sisters, took turns around the clock and sat at his bedside speaking to Steve, reminding him of past events, reading to him, and playing his favorite music. About two months later, when he regained consciousness, Steve was able to remember bits and pieces of their spoken words, which brought tears to the eyes of all who were present. Eventually, when his physical condition permitted, Steve was moved to a local rehabilitation hospital, where he came under the care of a renowned physiatrist who practiced a specialty sometimes referred to as rehabilitative medicine. Most unique about this particular doctor is that as a result of a childhood accident, he had been a quadriplegic since the age of twelve. Despite having very limited use of his hands, after medical school, residency, and board certification, he slowly rose to become a leader in his specialty and was the head of his department. Under his care, Steve slowly regained almost all of his gross motor skills, although he lacked the ability to perform many of the fine motor skills that you and I take for granted. For example, he could button his shirt, but he could not sew a button onto that same shirt. Although he achieved a high level of daily functioning and was trained to make many adjustments to carry out the activities of daily living, it became clear that Steve could never live alone. He had to depend on lists in order to remember to do things. For example, he could remember to prepare all that he needed to make bacon and eggs for breakfast but could forget to turn off the toaster, and as a result, he could burn the house down.

In addition to his physical limitations, the damage to his brain left Steve with short-term memory deficits. While he often demonstrated the ability to remember much about his past, his ability to remember current events was markedly limited. Series of tests carried out by neuropsychologists were able to pinpoint the areas of the brain that were damaged. These tests measure intellectual ability, hand-eye coordination, and other physical functions. Doctors are able to correlate their findings with the results of brain scans and other tests to confirm the areas of brain damage so various therapists can retrain other parts of the brain to take over the functions of the damaged areas that can never be restored. All of this was done at a long-term rehabilitation facility in Florida, where many such facilities are located for the simple fact that their costs of operation are significantly less than in the northeastern part of the country, where pay scales, land, and building costs are higher. Fortunately, Steve's mom and dad had a home in Florida, so when he moved to that long-term facility, they sold their home in New York and made Florida their state of residency.

When further therapy was no longer expected to result in improvements to Steve's physical or mental abilities, his mom and dad made significant modifications to their home to accommodate him. While the health care providers made tremendous progress in helping to restore Steve's ability to function, I found his level of functioning extremely troubling. While some may disagree, it seemed to me that Steve was like an animal locked in a cage, not in a zoo but in the middle of the wild. Although protected from attack, he could see what was around him and all that his life had been. While his needs were taken care of, he had also regained enough intellectual ability to fully understand all that he had lost, so he desperately wanted to regain his abilities. He was the proverbial boy in a bubble. Compare this to a patient who, while in a comatose state, has little idea of his surroundings and even less understanding of what life has to offer. Fortunately, this is a choice that most of us never have to make.

Well, Steve and his mom and dad did. While both cherished the time that they had together, there came a time when everyone concluded that life had something better to offer. To a degree consistent with his ability, Steve wanted to be on his own. His mom and dad wanted to do whatever made him happy. Together, they studied their options and came up with the best of all worlds. There are living facilities that, while offering separate living quarters, provide group activities and a degree of supervision less intrusive than Steve found while living with his mom and dad. Fortunately, one such facility was also located in Florida, about an hour's drive from his parents' home. With heavy hearts, almost like sending a child off to school for the first time, his family moved Steve to that facility. It proved to be the right choice, and Steve, as of the last time I had contact, had found his place in life.

During all this time, Steve was never able to regain any memory of the accident, and so as I prepared to represent him in court, I was left to my own devices to handle the lawsuit. To use the word lucky when applied to Steve's accident is difficult, but in some respects, it was appropriate. The truck borrowed by the lumber company had what at that time was the minimum amount of liability insurance permitted under law, $10,000. Since the accident occurred while Ed was in the course of his employment, the liability insurance policy that covered its vehicles came next and provided coverage in the amount of $100,000. Combined, these two policies were insufficient to compensate Steve for his injuries and the lifetime of expenses to care for him. Luckily, the lumber company also maintained what is known as an umbrella policy, with additional liability coverage of $2.5 million. My job was to force these three companies, which would probably pay nothing if they could get away with it, to pay him all that money.

Having represented insurance companies in the role of defense in accident cases during my career, I had the advantage of knowing how they thought about things. The injuries were so severe, there was nothing they could do or say to diminish the value of the case. This was true despite the fact that Steve had an IQ of about ninety (on the lower end of average) before the accident and never was going to be a rocket scientist. The only hope that the insurance carriers had was to try to prove, under the law applicable to accident cases known as comparative negligence, that Steve was in whole or in part responsible for the accident. By way of example, if they could prove that he was 50 percent at fault for the accident and their clients were also 50 percent at fault, Steve could collect only 50 percent of any jury award. Of necessity, I had to concentrate on doing two things—either prove that the defendants were 100 percent at fault, or prove to a jury, in the event that Steve was partially at fault (using the 50 percent figure as a working thesis), that the fair compensation for his injuries exceeded twice the insurance coverage. While it is true that a plaintiff who is awarded an amount in excess of insurance coverage is entitled to collect the excess from the defendant's personal assets, investigation in this case revealed that the lumber company was in debt and the owner had little in his own name except his home, which he owned jointly with his wife.

After I was retained, I sent my best two investigators out, one after the other when I wasn't happy with the results of the first, to review all police and other medical responder records and to find not only witnesses to the accident but also the identity of the person who called 9-1-1. That person was so excited that he neglected to give his name, and a review of the 9-1-1 transmission revealed that the operator forgot to ask for the name, an error that cost her a thirty-day suspension. Once again, fed up with my high-priced private investigators, I set out to do my own investigation. Going out on a Saturday or Sunday, when most people are not at work, is always a good idea. I rang the bell of every home and apartment in the area of the accident and walked into every store and business. Saturday was a bust, but Sunday was a bonanza. The owner of a two-story, split-level home answered the door, and when I introduced myself, he said, "I was wondering when someone would be coming around." Apparently, one of my investigators had come to the house when he was at work but had never returned. (I didn't return that investigator's future calls for more work, either.) Not only had the witness seen the accident, he swore that he gave his name to one of the village police officers. He described the scene in detail, including the location of at least seventeen boards that had fallen from the truck, and I marked each location with chalk and took a photo of the whole scene. I then asked the witness whether he knew what happened to the wooden boards. He explained that in their rush to get the roadway open to traffic again, the police asked if anyone standing around would help move the boards out of the roadway. Most bystanders got into their cars and left or walked home to get ready for work. The witness, considering this an opportunity, made about seven trips to his nearby home, taking virtually all the boards he could to his backyard. I, of course, accepted his offer to see them, and when we got there, he explained that he used the boards as support for a new deck he built outside the upper level of his home.

As if leading me from dot to dot, he pointed out some remaining boards and pieces of board lying in a pile under the new porch. Already in shock, I still wasn't ready for the next thing he said: "By the way, do you want the board that went through the windshield and hit your client in the head?" Gasping for air, I had a vision of having to dismantle the new porch, when he went over to the wood pile and pulled out an intact board, covered with plastic at one end. He had done that to cover up the blood, brain fragments, and glass still embedded in the end of the board. It was only then that he mentioned the pictures he had taken before the boards were removed from the roadway. All of this physical evidence, together with a written statement I took from him and a later deposition during which he repeated what he saw and told me, left me with a sense of absolute confidence that a jury could only conclude that Steve was in no way at fault for the accident.

Having concluded virtually all pretrial discovery, my next hurdle was to try to get an early trial date. The problem was with the attorneys assigned to defend the case by the insurance carrier with the $10,000 policy. Since that carrier was first in line for any recovery, its attorneys controlled the defense.

The attorneys were what is known as outside counsel, a firm hired by the insurance carrier and paid an hourly rate to defend the case. Since this carrier had only $10,000 to lose, it was an outside attorney's dream. They could run up the bills and never make an offer, since once they put up their carrier's money, they might get replaced by the next carrier's attorneys. Trying to overcome this roadblock, I requested a conference with the judge, whom I respected as a practical, sensible man with an innate ability to get to the heart of a problem. Unfortunately, you had to get past his less competent law clerk to see him. Although the other attorneys failed to show, the clerk allowed me to explain why I was there anyway. I explained the lineup of insurance policies and said I wanted the judge to direct that a conference be scheduled at which the judge should direct that all of the carriers' claims representatives be present. Only then would the stalling stop and real settlement discussions begin. The law clerk then came up with his own "solution."

"Why not settle with the carrier that has the $10,000 policy and get them out of the way?" he reasoned. I didn't have the intestinal fortitude to explain to him that if I released the owner of the vehicle from the case, under law, it would constitute a release of all defendants, leaving me as the only defendant, since I would be guilty in a legal malpractice case of unparalleled stupidity. Instead, I simply told him that we weren't communicating and said I would sit there all day if necessary to see the judge.

It turned out that the judge was in his private chambers all along, and when he opened the door and saw me, he invited me into his chambers. I told him that I wanted to speak privately, so he asked the law clerk to leave, although he did not completely close the door. I explained my reason for being there and my discussion with his law clerk. He walked over to the door, closed it, and then, in not very judicious language, explained his frustration at other mistakes the clerk had made during his two-month tenure with the judge. He went on to explain that his political party forced the clerk's appointment on him but that he was ready to fire him, regardless of the consequences. Next, in what I perceived to be a serious tone, he asked me if I was interested in the job. I respectfully turned him down, indicating that I couldn't afford the loss of earnings, at which he laughed and dropped the subject.

Agreeing with my plan of action, he called his law clerk in and directed that he communicate with all lawyers and carriers and schedule the meeting I was seeking. Two weeks later, when the meeting was held and the judge got nowhere in his effort to forge a settlement, he did something even more than I could have hoped for. He asked for a list of the out-of-state health care providers that I intended to call as witnesses, all of whom lived in Florida. He directed that all such witnesses be allowed to testify by videotape in lieu of personal appearances at trial. Then came the coup de grâce. This conference was on a Tuesday. He directed that all attorneys be prepared to travel to Florida by Thursday to conduct depositions and that no one return until they were concluded. He indicated that if any legal issues arose requiring that a ruling be made by him, the parties should call and he would interrupt anything he was doing to make the ruling. He also directed that he be advised of the progress being made by 4:30 P.M. each day. Finally, in a ruling that clearly demonstrated his annoyance at the insurance companies for their intransigence, he also directed that upon our return, we be ready to begin jury selection within three days.

Having been promised full cooperation by all facilities in Florida, since the staff had all come to love Steve and his family, I was able to immediately line up five of the therapists I needed for the videotaped depositions, as well as the two physicians whose testimony I also wanted. These depositions took six days surrounding a weekend. I had to buy extra clothing. The other attorneys never stopped complaining. Each deposition put the defendants deeper in the hole, so each morning the offer, which started at $10,000, went up, so that by the time we returned to New York, the offer was up to $1,510,000. I never wavered from my demand of all of the insurance dollars. Just before jury selection, the offer went up to $2,110,000. With interest rates at a high for the year of 15 percent, the ability to take advantage of Florida's tax-free investments for residents, and to put a major portion of the settlement funds into an annuity that would pay Steve tax-free money for the rest of his life, his Dad, who was a sophisticated investment expert, decided to accept the settlement, since he understood how much it would cost to try the case and didn't want to put Steve through the experience of living through a trial. When expenses were later computed, I found that I had spent approximately $83,000 in bringing the case to the eve of trial. It was worth it, not only for the money but for the opportunity to make a profound difference in the lives of Steve and his family. Looking back, while each case may have contributed to my now fully grey head of hair and beard, I wear my war scars proudly. It's easy to understand why, to some trial attorneys, cane in hand, retirement is out of the question.

They Turn on Their Own Like Rats

I first met Walter Michaels through an attorney for whom I did trial work.

Walter was a good man to know, since he was the regional manager for a major bodily injury liability insurance company that conducted business throughout the United States. In his position as regional manager, Walter had direct supervision over seven offices within the region, with each office employing about seventy-five people, including secretarial staff, support staff, claims people, underwriters, supervisory personnel, and a legal department. Although he himself was not an attorney, Walter could hold his own in matters concerning policy interpretation and the laws that applied to various aspects of liability litigation. He supervised a budget in excess of $60 million.

Walter had also attended just about every seminar offered by the company concerning injuries, medical treatment, pharmaceuticals, and the calling of expert witnesses, including physicians, either to prove or disprove the existence, or lack thereof, of injuries and their long-term effect upon the activities of daily living. It is not a stretch to say that he could have successfully applied for, and graduated from, medical school.

The events that led up to Walter's accident are, to say the least, coincidental. The insurance company that Walter worked for had just moved into a new suite of about forty thousand square feet, located within a newly constructed luxury building that had been built by one of the leading contractors in the area. The decision to move into the building was made, in part, because Walter's employer was selected to insure the building.

Who could have ever foreseen that about two weeks after moving to the building, Walter, while using the men's room, would slip on liquid soap on the floor? Who could have foreseen that the fall would cause him to sustain three compression fractures of the lumbar spine, resulting in a permanent disability that prevented him from ever returning to work?

When I was contacted by Walter several days after the accident, I was flattered—no, make that awed—since there were so many highly qualified personal injury attorneys in the area. He explained to me that he and another attorney, Vincent Barnes, a friend of Walter's, had conferred about the selection of his attorney. Luckily, Vincent did not do any trial work, instead referring his trial work to a trial attorney like me, and they jointly decided to retain my services. Walter explained that he had always been impressed with my handling of cases in which the defendant was insured by his employer. They both knew of my background as an attorney who both prosecuted and defended personal injury cases, as well as my investigative skills; I was a natural for the case.

Knowing that a thorough investigation is often the key to success, I immediately went into action. The next day, I met with Walter and had him give me the pants that he was wearing when the accident occurred. Sure enough, there was a stain on one of the pant legs consistent with Walter's description of his fall. We then went to the men's room along with Steve Franks, an employee of Walter's, who had come into the bathroom and found him on the floor, writhing in pain. Further examination offered a clue to the cause of the accident; the liquid hand soap that filled the dispensers, when spilled on the tile floor, created a slippery condition similar to an ice skating rink. This was observed by Steve Franks.

We took a sample and then got into contact with the cleaning company that filled the dispensers and learned that they had been filled earlier that morning. Walter's pants, along with the sample soap, were sent over to an expert for chemical analysis, and sure enough, there was a match.

Based upon this investigation, as well as other preliminary work, legal action was commenced against the owner of the building as well as against the cleaning company. State law prevented a suit against Walter's employer; his sole remedy against it was a worker's compensation claim, which was also initiated.

It is worthy of note that each year, all employees of the company were given a written evaluation, which was placed in their personnel file. For ten straight years prior to the accident, Walter had received a rating of ten out of ten, the best rating provided by the company. Six months after the accident, the first time a claim could be filed, I also filed an application for Social Security disability benefits on Walter's behalf, alleging that he was permanently and totally disabled from any form of gainful employment. As part of the evaluation process, Walter was examined by an independent medical expert who agreed with Walter's doctor that he was indeed disabled. This application is rarely granted after initial application. Well, surprise, surprise, after the usual seven-month processing period, the initial application was granted, retroactive to the date of the accident. The next step was to determine the monthly benefits, computed upon the total quarters paid into the system and the amount paid. In the case of a veteran, an additional allowance for active duty is made.

All this was considered when Walter's monthly entitlement was computed. I was shown a document containing an abstract of Walter's military record, including his military I.D. number, and his Social Security number—evidence that will figure into the case later on.

While the legal action was pending and during pretrial discovery, we were served with Walter's last yearly personnel evaluation. Wouldn't you know it? Walter's evaluation had dropped to 3.5, raising questions about his effectiveness and ability to continue in his position with the company. Clearly, this determination was going to be the company's way of minimizing a claim for future lost earnings by lessening his value to the company. It was no surprise that the other shoe dropped about three months later, when he received a Notice of Termination, citing unsatisfactory performance beginning about three months before the accident as a reason for his termination. The first blemish on his otherwise perfect record. Boy, it's great to know your employer has your back in your time of need, isn't it?

We then amended the complaint to include a claim against his employer for wrongful discharge, creating a rare instance in which the building owner's insurance company (also Walter's employer) became a named party to the lawsuit.

As part of my discovery demands, I called upon the insurance company to produce a copy of Steve Franks's written statement, which he said the company had asked him to provide. That statement, which helped us, was admissible at trial as a business record. Again, it was no surprise when the insurance company denied that any such statement was taken. It then fired Steve Franks, a twenty-five-year employee, questioning whether any such statement was ever made. Fortunately, Franks had kept a copy of his statement, and the copy was admitted into evidence at the trial. The defendants also exercised their right to have a physical examination of Walter and, as expected, they selected a well-known neurologist who questioned whether the injuries were disabling, as claimed, or whether Walter was faking his injuries, given his insurance background. Talk about rats turning on their own! Not surprisingly, the case was not settled after discovery was completed, and it came up for a jury trial about two years after the accident. The insurance company brought in its chief litigation counsel from out of state, and the carrier for the cleaning company brought in its best local litigator.

After jury selection, we were assigned to the senior justice of the court, who directed, on my application, that the trial not be bifurcated, meaning that all issues of liability and damages would be tried at one time. A plaintiff makes that request when he believes that the severity of the injury may prejudice the jury in his favor. Through my first witness, Steve Franks, I was able to get his copy of his statement admitted into evidence, which made his employer, the insurance company, appear the villain, having fired him and accused him of lying about the content of the statement or that the statement was ever made. The next witness called was the defendant's medical expert, who was called out of turn because he was going out of the country. Not only was Dr. Peters a well-respected professional, he was also an experienced expert witness who boasted that he had never been successfully cross-examined. Although his testimony was very effective on the medical issues, especially in regard to his contention that Walter's injuries were not as disabling as claimed, perhaps in his haste to leave the country, the doctor hadn't discovered the name of Walter's treating physician.

The first thing I did when I got up, after saying "Good morning" to Dr. Peters, was to indicate to him that I was pleased to see that he was no longer walking with a limp. The doctor sat silently with a quizzical look on his face. Clearly, he never saw what was coming. I then asked, "Doctor, isn't it a fact that about a year ago, you suffered a compound fracture of your left leg?"

His response, "Well, yes," was nearly drowned out by the objections raised by both defense counsels. Fortunately, the trial judge, not seeing where I was going, overruled the objection, believing this to be idle banter.

My next question offered a hint of what was to come: "And doctor, isn't it a fact that out of the twenty-five to fifty thousand doctors you had to select from, you selected Dr. Harry Samuels to treat your badly fractured leg?"

"When the doctor answered "Yes," I wish I had a picture of the expression on the faces of both defense counsels, for they both now knew what was about to happen, as did the medical expert.

"Doctor," I continued, "did you know that Dr. Harry Samuels was the treating orthopedist in this case, and that he furnished a report disagreeing with you regarding the severity of the injury, and that he opined that Walter is in fact permanently and severely injured and will never be able to return to work as a result thereof?"

Of course, Dr. Peters had to admit that he was not aware that his own doctor (and, as it turned out, his good friend) was the treating physician and that Dr. Samuels had diametrically opposing views of the plaintiff's injuries.

"By the way, doctor, given your respect for Dr. Samuels, wouldn't you also agree that this jury should give great weight to Dr. Samuels's opinions in this case, even though they may differ with yours?"

When Dr. Peters agreed and said "Yes," I nearly collapsed into my chair. As Jackie Gleason would say, "How sweet it is!"

I've never gotten a straight answer from Dr. Peters as to whether he told his good friend, Dr. Samuels, that I knew about their relationship, but by the end of the trial, did it really matter?

The next witness was the expert chemist, whose testimony was, without question, unassailable. The only cross-examination available to the defense was to question whether the stain was put on the pants by the plaintiff. Once again, this attack did not sit well with the jury.

In case you are wondering, it is usually a good trial tactic to put your plaintiff on the stand as late in the plaintiff's case as you can. While witnesses, on application of either party, are usually excluded from the courtroom to prevent their echoing another witness's testimony, the parties to a lawsuit have a constitutional right to be in the courtroom at all times, enabling a party to hear and see the testimony of all witnesses.

Riding high, I put Walter on the stand and proceeded to lay out his life history to the jury, from childhood to schooling; then from his military history to marriage and fatherhood; then through his work history, both before and after his starting with the insurance company, including his education though company seminars. I moved on to the details regarding the accident and, finally, to his life since the accident to the day of trial, later to be supported by calling Dr. Samuels to the stand. It is hard to imagine a better witness than Walter, who, by word and body language, held the attention of the jury throughout his testimony.

The first cross-examination by the attorney for the insurance company, while professionally done, really went nowhere. It was done in what I refer to as an A-to-Z manner. Go over all the testimony from direct examination and hope to develop an inconsistency. Sometimes the technique works, but if it doesn't, the result is to have the jury hear the same things again, which can reinforce the party's credibility in the minds of the jurors. Fortunately, Walter remembered my general admonition in which I likened a trial to a basketball game. Unlike in baseball, you never win a basketball game by a shutout. The other team will score points. Let them. Show no emotion and NEVER look over to me for help. That only reinforces the damage.

One down and one to go, I thought, as the other attorney for the building owner got up and appeared to be utilizing the same cross-examination technique. Since I had the benefit of speaking to him later, I am sure that what occurred next was something he happened to ask without realizing the significance. He showed Walter an employment application he had filled out for the insurance company. In it, Walter had listed a four-year employment with a company that seemed to conflict with the years Walter had testified that he was in the Army, including paratrooper school. I thought, at first, that maybe Walter had forgotten to tell me about an injury to his back during that training. You could see the meltdown as Walter mumbled something that I didn't hear, and then he started crying. The judge immediately asked Walter if he wanted a break, but to my surprise he said no, and then, over the next few minutes, proceeded to tell the following story. He admitted that he had lied about his military service because he was classified as 4-F due to a heart murmur, which would have precluded him from service in the armed forces, and he said he was ashamed to tell his children about it. With that over with, the attorney asked whether Walter had ever really worked for the company listed in the application. It was then that Walter turned to the judge and asked for a short recess.

I must admit that when I walked into a private conference room with Walter, I was beyond confused. I knew that Walter was in the Army because I had seen the documentation during the Social Security application. "What the hell is going on here, Walter?" I yelled loudly, knocking over a chair in the process. It caused such a racket that a court officer rushed in, thinking he was going to break up a fight. The story I was told by Walter cannot be related in full for reasons that will become clear. He proceeded to tell me that he was, in fact, in the Army; that he went through almost all of paratrooper school; but that before he finished, he was recruited by a special branch. After completing aptitude and psychological evaluations, Walter was removed from active duty, his military records were sealed, and he became an operative for a paramilitary group which will remain unnamed. He was given special weapons training and became what he called a "wet operative," a label that I had never heard of before but later came to understand to mean an assassin. He went on to relate operations he was involved in out of the country in places like Vietnam, Laos, Cambodia, and East Germany. He also explained that the company listed on the work application was a government shell company used to fund the operation. He also told me about "wet" operations within the United States, which, having a political overtone, I must decline to discuss.

I asked Walter if it was possible to call someone from the "special branch" to explain all this in private to the judge. His response: that "we would cease to exist" and that he was covered by the Espionage Act. I must admit, this information sent a chill up my spine. The look on Walter's face, particularly his eyes, was piercing, when he told me point-blank: "Settle the case. Whatever the offer, settle the case." I went back to the judge *in camera* (privately), and, in the best way I could, explained my dilemma to him. It was then that the judge, who had an extensive military background, told me that he had a feeling that it was something like this. He also told me that what Walter had muttered, which I was unable to hear, was, "I knew that someday this was going to come back to haunt me."

The case was settled for the outstanding offer of $200,000. The defense counsel was never told what had happened and, as far as I know, the judge told them nothing about our conversation. As is my custom, I spoke to the jury later and they told me that Walter's lying to his kids would not have affected them, and several asked me if $2 million would have been enough.

Several years later, I became friendly with a ranking member of the CIA. Without divulging Walter's name, I related the substance of the story and asked him if it was possible, advising him that this took place during the Eisenhower and Kennedy presidencies. At his request, I gave him Walter's Social Security number and he said that he would get back to me, only to advise whether Walter had ever been in the Army. When he did, his answer was terse and to the point. "Leave it alone," he said. I did as he asked until now, after learning of Walter's death a couple of years ago, which, to the best of my knowledge, was due to natural causes. They say that sometimes the truth is stranger than fiction. I leave it to you to decide.

What Were They Thinking?

Many New York attorneys, when they are first starting out, try their hand at accepting 18B assignments, which are cases in which the lawyer's fee is capped because the defendant has few assets. By now, you all know that those accused of a crime have the right to an attorney. If they truly cannot afford one, they have the right to have an attorney assigned to them by the local Legal Aid Society. Those who are accused are interviewed by Legal Aid and, if they qualify, are afforded a defense attorney free of charge. If they don't qualify because they are found to have too much income or too many assets, many accused still do not have the wherewithal to afford a private attorney. That is where the 18B panel comes in.

A private attorney can seek admission to the 18B panel and, if deemed qualified, his or her name is added to a list, which is available to the criminal court judges, who then will assign a panel member to defend the accused if the judge believes the defendant will not qualify for Legal Aid but cannot afford a private attorney. The member of the 18B panel is then paid a set fee per hour by the panel with funds from a county agency.

When the 18B attorney meets the accused, if he or she decides to take the case, the attorney and the accused may agree that the attorney will be paid a modest fee to supplement the money paid by the panel to the attorney. At the end of the case, the attorney submits a time sheet and is paid at a fixed hourly rate. That time sheet is signed by the attorney and the client and then reviewed by the judge, and if it is deemed in order by the judge, he or she signs an order fixing the fee, which the attorney then submits to the panel for payment. If the client has not paid all of the remaining fee, it's up to the attorney to try to collect the fee, which the client often does not pay since he or she cannot afford it, in which case you can't get blood from a stone. At the time of the case I'm about to tell you about, the hourly fee was $30, which, while meager, can add up if the attorney takes enough assignments.

I took this case under unusual circumstances. My excellent success rate was the reason the head of the 18B panel in one of the five New York City boroughs called one day and asked whether I would come in to see him, which I of course did. He was basically honest in explaining to me that there was an assignment he wanted me to take and that it required someone willing to take on a difficult client. That turned out to be an understatement. He went on to explain that five other attorneys had previously taken on the client, only to quickly ask that they be released from the assignment, waiving their fee for work already done. All of this had come about after the client, following psychiatric evaluation by a court-appointed doctor, had been determined to be a paranoid schizophrenic with homicidal tendencies. Somehow, without the benefit of the client recieving any psychiatric treatment other than psychotropic medication, a sixth psychiatrist examined him and found him to be free of any psychosis and fit to stand trial.

The problem was that after spending time with him in a cell at the detention center, none of the other attorneys who had been assigned would get back into a cell or be anywhere near him out of fear for their life. The charges he faced were attempted murder with a deadly weapon, a felony, and interference with governmental administration, a misdemeanor. At first blush, the second charge sounded minor, until I learned that it stemmed from an incident when he was in a bathroom at the detention center and refused to return to his cell. When the guards tried to force him back to his cell, he pulled a urinal off the wall with his bare hands and proceeded to beat the guards with it until he was subdued with Mace, with the assistance of several more guards.

I was ready to say no when I got the pep talk, during which the head of the panel reminded me that I had been so highly recommended by my former partner, the Commish, who told him how good and tough I was. Then came the sweetener: if I took the assignment, I could select ten more "choice assignments" and walk out with these files that day. Usually it would take two to three months to get ten assignments, and each might not pay much. When he also agreed that I could keep the ten assignments even if I decided to give back this bad one, we struck a deal. Please keep in mind that at that point I had never seen nor met the defendant, Ahmed Cortese. Was I in for a shock!

Knowing that there was a court date scheduled a week later, I made it my business to see my new client about three days later. As I entered the detention center, I showed my attorney's card and advised the guard at the entrance who I was there to see. I was surprised to hear the guard say that the warden wanted to see me, which was a first. I was escorted to the warden's office and, after he introduced himself and confirmed that I was the assigned 18B counsel, he expressed how happy he was that new counsel had been assigned. He went on to explain that Ahmed had been there for about twelve months and that he couldn't wait for him to leave. He indicated that in his fifteen years as the warden, he never had an inmate like Ahmed. He explained that the prisoner was being held on the eighth floor, in the south ward, and that all of the other inmates were afraid of him. He said there was a television in the ward, but no one would sit in the room with Ahmed because he wouldn't permit anyone else to touch the channel selector or adjust the sound. He also related the story about him tearing the urinal off the wall and added that the two guards he was initially hitting with it had applied for a transfer to another facility. No guard wanted to be near him without at least two other guards present. "Please," begged the warden, "get him out of here as fast as you can."

When I was escorted to the eighth floor, Ahmed was already sitting in the interview room with his back to the door. The guards unlocked the door, wished me well, and locked me in with him. When I introduced myself, he got up, turned to face me, and held out his hand to greet me. It's hard to describe my first impression, except to say that I was wondering why he was wearing football pads until I realized that that was all him under that sweatshirt. He was about six feet, four inches tall, about 250 pounds of solid muscle, and the hand that I reached out to shake had fingers as long as I had ever seen. I later learned that he had shed about thirty pounds while incarcerated. He did, however, have a mild voice and was polite and happy to hear that I was his new attorney and that his case was marked for trial now that the psychiatrist had found him mentally fit to participate in his defense.

Ahmed then went on to explain his side of the story. It seems that he was living with his common-law wife for about nine months when he discovered that she was going to a crack house to smoke drugs. Apparently incensed that the operator of the crack house, whom he knew, would allow her to be there without his permission, Ahmed went there to clear the air. An argument broke out, during which the drug dealer fell on a chair, which broke. Ahmed was in the process of beating the drug dealer with a piece of the chair when the dealer tried to bite him. Ahmed broke the dealer's jaw and tried his best to rip his jaw off before leaving when he heard that someone had called the cops. When arrested, he pled not guilty and said he had acted in self-defense, not denying that he was there to stop his wife's drug use. He indicated that he and his wife had since split up and that he did not know where she was. He could not or did not give me the names of any witnesses and did not know where the complainant lived after he got out of the hospital, where he remained for about five weeks after the fight.

OK, I can handle this, I thought to myself, until he started to explain that since he'd been in the detention center, he had become convinced that his actions and thoughts were being controlled by the mayor through wires that extended from City Hall, about three blocks away, which were somehow attached to his head, although you couldn't see or feel them. As he explained this, his eyes were beginning to roll. All of this convinced me that I would never again, of my own free will, sit in a locked cell alone with this very huge and extremely intimidating man, so after telling him that I would see him in court in a week, in a very shaky voice, I asked the guards to get me out of there. As I left, I think I heard something about a bet between the guards as to whether I was going to be able to walk out of the cell under my own power. I wonder if the guard who bet yes had to give odds.

Aware that the case would be a challenge, to say the least, I undertook an investigation and learned that the police had been unable to recover any portion of the broken chair, which was the alleged deadly weapon. I also learned that three weeks after the arrest, which was about three days after the incident, the arresting officer had been shot in the stomach and had been out on disability until about three days before my visit with Ahmed. When I next met

Ahmed in court, he was brought in wearing shackles. The court officers explained to me that Ahmed could break out of handcuffs, so they required the use of shackles to move him. He did not speak to me in court, although he was mumbling something, which may have been a conversation with the mayor, but who am I to interrupt? The case was marked ready for trial.

My adversary was about my age, had spent four years with the D.A.'s office, and went on to become one of its finest major felony attorneys. I'm glad we clashed early in his career.

My instinct that the prosecution really wasn't ready for the trial, in part due to the shooting of the detective who was the arresting officer, turned out to be correct. The detective testified that he tried to retrieve the alleged weapon from the apartment where the incident occurred but was unable to because the landlord wouldn't let him in, an explanation that caused some of the jurors to sneer in disbelief. The fact that he never returned with a warrant permitting him entry didn't go over well either. When I asked him whether the police would have taken the landlord's no for an answer if they thought the gun that he had been shot with was in the apartment, the look on his face was the only answer I needed.

The complainant's testimony was no better. His difficulty talking was due to both of his temporomandibular joints, the hinges connecting his lower jaw to his skull, having been fractured. That they never quite healed was no help. Despite his injuries, the jury had no sympathy for the drug dealer and probably felt he had gotten what he deserved. I did not put Ahmed on the stand. First, there was no need to, and second, since I never talked to him again after our interview in the detention center, I couldn't put a client on the stand when I didn't know what he was going to say. I was also afraid that the "mayor" might take the stand with him.

I did not care about the misdemeanor charge for several reasons. First, there was no defense. Second, it was a misdemeanor, which is punishable by no more than a year in jail, and he had already spent thirteen months in the detention center. If he were found guilty, the most he could be sentenced to was time served. Also, a careful check by my investigator and by the warden indicated that there were no holds on him, meaning that if he was found not guilty of the felony charge, even if he was found guilty on the lesser charge, the judge would have no choice but to set him free.

It took the jury only thirty-five minutes of deliberation after they came back from their free lunch to report their verdict: not guilty of attempted murder; guilty of interference with governmental administration for beating the guards with the urinal. I moved for his immediate release. I was surprised when the judge, instead of ordering his unconditional release, directed that a probation report be prepared, and he adjourned the case for six weeks so that the probation department could prepare it. I reminded the judge that since the defendant was entitled to be credited with time served, there could be no probation, but I couldn't change his mind. As for Ahmed's release, the judge indicated that he would sign the order of release only after the warden assured him that there were no outstanding holds or warrants to justify retaining him. The judge remanded him to the detention center, pending the report by the warden. Ahmed seemed to understand when I explained everything and peaceably sat as he was again shackled for his return to detention.

I immediately went to the detention center. Word had already filtered back to the warden, who was so happy that when he hugged me, I thought he was also going to kiss me. I told him that I would not go to the cell to advise Ahmed of his release until I had the judge's order. The warden already had the report ready for the judge, and I took it back to the court, and the judge signed it. I then went back to Ahmed's cell and advised him of his imminent release, reminding him that he had to return to court in six weeks. He assured me that he would return, and a half hour later, to the delight of the warden and the guards, he walked out a free man. I kidded around and asked the warden and guards if they would throw him a victory party. I'm not sure they appreciated my sense of humor.

Anyone familiar with the case was ready to give me odds that he would not return to court on the agreed-upon date. I was absolutely shocked when he entered the courtroom and calmly sat down next to me and shook my hand. When the case was called, we stepped up to counsel table, as did my adversary. After the judge looked at the papers in front of him and then looked up, I said, "Judge, I assume that you are ready to sentence my client to time served."

The judge motioned counsel to approach the bench. He then said to me, "Counsel, something has come to my attention. Perhaps you should both return to counsel table and I will explain."

As I turned around to return to my table, I noticed that the entire courtroom was now surrounded by at least fifteen court officers, who had quietly entered the courtroom while I was at the bench. The judge then proceeded to explain that an error had occurred, discovered only a day before. It seemed that Ahmed, at the time of the incident, was on parole, arising from a federal conviction for armed robbery with a shotgun, for which he had served seven years of a ten-year sentence. The court was advised by the federal prosecutor that he intended to initiate a violation of probation proceeding based on Ahmed's conviction on the misdemeanor and had issued a warrant for his immediate arrest.

The court officers approached Ahmed to take him into custody. It is hard to describe the next fifteen minutes in the courtroom as anything but mayhem. I can only offer a general report, since I spent the better part of that time hiding under the counsel table, fearing for my life. There were uniformed bodies flying all over the courtroom as these basically out-of-shape court officers tried to tackle Ahmed in order to get him to the ground to shackle him. In those days, court officers were neither armed nor allowed to carry Mace, nor any weapon for that matter. It was only by reason of fatigue from fighting off the total weight of fifteen men that the officers finally were able to subdue and shackle him, and order was restored. After he was removed from the courtroom, the judge asked me if I was going to the jail to see Ahmed. I asked the judge, "My God, what were you thinking? Why didn't you give me warning of what was going to happen? Maybe I could have spoken to him and explained. I had his trust. You have to be crazy to think that I would ever get back into a cell with that man." I never got a straight answer from the judge. The only thing I remember is his asking me whether I was going to continue representing Ahmed.

Not only did I tell him no, I also asked him to sign an immediate order releasing me from any further obligation to represent Ahmed, telling the judge that I was waiving my fee and would not be submitting any application for reimbursement for expenses. Part of my disgust was the fact that if I had been informed that there was a possibility of a violation of probation, I would have attempted to defend the lesser charge, since it was conviction on that charge which led to the violation proceeding. On that basis, which was a gross miscarriage of justice in my opinion, I asked that the judge set aside the conviction, which he refused to do. At least the prosecutor had the decency to acknowledge the logic of my argument, and he said he would consider rethinking his position when a new attorney took over the case.

Readers may wonder why I would fight so hard for the rights of a person who seemed to be dangerous and delusional. Let me remind them that one of the pillars of our legal system is that all defendants are entitled to an attorney.

A week later, after much thought, I notified the 18B panel of my resignation. For this much aggravation, I figured, I might as well get paid and be able to select my clients. Before I forget, a story about the melee appeared in the newspapers the next day. Personally, I think it should have appeared in the sports section. I'm a fight fan, and I haven't seen many better, even in Madison Square Garden.

When in Doubt, Spell It Out

To the best of my recollection, it was in the third grade, when we were learning about abbreviation, that the teacher taught us a little jingle: "When in doubt, write it out." If only the EMT at the scene of this accident had learned the same jingle, an awful lot of trouble might have been saved and a gross miscarriage of justice would not have had the chance of occurring.

It was a cold February morning at about 2:10 A.M. when my client, Frank Marino, was suddenly awakened from a deep sleep. Fortunately, he was used to that happening. For the prior seven years, as a volunteer fireman, it was not unusual for him to get a telephone call, or if he was up and his scanner was on, for him to hear the firehouse put out a call that necessitated his immediate response. In this instance, the call was to respond to a fire in a warehouse less than four miles from his home on the south side of eastern Long Island. Frank jumped into his clothes, which were always on a stand near his bed, kissed his wife goodbye in response to her usual, "Be careful; I love you," and scooted out to his car. It always faced the roadway in order to save time, as seconds could sometimes mean an eternity in the case of a serious injury. As Frank pulled into the roadway, making a left turn, he switched on the blue emergency light on his dashboard. Although the light gave him no special privilege as a motorist on the roadway, most motorists understood the light to signify that an emergency responder was on the way to help someone in need and would yield the right of way. Even at an intersection, the emergency responder was usually shown courtesy to enable him to safely proceed to the aid of another.

Unknown to Frank, a county police officer in a marked patrol car was proceeding in an easterly direction on a major east-west thoroughfare, also responding to the fire. One of the major issues presented at trial was whether the officer had turned on his siren and emergency lights, or whether, because of the time of night and the good road lighting, he was proceeding with only his regular headlights on. As Frank proceeded in a northerly direction toward that roadway, at a point only about eight blocks from his home, he was going downhill, and heavy shrubbery blocked his view to the left. He planned to make a left turn in order to head three more blocks to the firehouse, and he heard nothing as he approached the uncontrolled intersection. The police car, coming toward that intersection, on the other hand, was intending to go straight, since he was responding directly to the site of the fire, which was located several blocks further east. As Frank entered the intersection, the police car, going in excess of sixty miles per hour, hit the driver's side of Frank's truck broadside, with sufficient force that Frank's truck was knocked about twelve feet to the east before flipping over and landing on its roof. Fortunately, Frank's seat belt prevented him from being ejected from his truck. The police officer was knocked unconscious and suffered a broken leg, but none of the injuries were life-threatening, and he was able to return to work in about three months.

Unfortunately, the same cannot be said about Frank. After using a device known as the Jaws of Life to extricate him from his mangled truck, it was quickly determined that Frank lacked feeling in his legs and was unable to wiggle his toes. His neck was immediately immobilized; he was tied to a stretcher and taken to the trauma center of the local teaching hospital. An X-ray, MRI, and CAT scan examination revealed that Frank had sustained fractures at three cervical disc levels, and although there was a lot of swelling and a small tear of the spinal cord, there was cautious optimism that with proper care, he might regain some use of his legs. His head was placed in a device known as a halo brace, which is round and is held in place by screws that are kept in place by drilling screw holes into the skull. It is intended to prevent even the slightest movement of the head and neck, and the screws are regularly adjusted to prevent any rotation as well. The degree of pain and discomfort, between the fractures and the halo device, has been described as unbearable by those who have ever endured this treatment.

Application of the halo followed six hours of extensive, delicate surgery to correct the fractured vertebrae and to help reduce the swelling to prevent further damage to the spinal cord. Given the involvement of the patrol car in the accident, a thorough accident investigation was conducted, including taking numerous photographs. Not conducted by the police was something referred to as an accident reconstruction, which is usually conducted by an engineer with training, experience, and expertise in this field. Fortunately, this case was referred to me by an attorney who at one time was one of the best personal injury attorneys in the area. Years before, he had moved into the commercial litigation field. About three weeks before the accident, I was in trial for several days in the local Supreme Court, and I noticed the referring attorney sitting in the courtroom on several occasions during the trial. Several days later, he telephoned and asked to see me. During our discussion, he indicated that he was no longer satisfied with the attorney to which his firm had been referring their trial work and asked if I was interested in handling that work, contingent on me paying them a referral fee, which is common in this area of law. I was thrilled, considering his reputation in the field. I never expected his call, so soon after that conversation, during which he told me about Frank's accident and asked me to handle the case.

It was fortunate that, as experienced attorneys, we were both on the same page and agreed upon the necessity of immediately hiring an accident reconstruction expert to guard against any prejudice by the police department during its investigation. I called in an expert I had used before and within twenty-four hours had him at the scene of the accident, where I furnished him with the reports and photographs my investigator, a retired policeman, had already managed to obtain copies of through his sources. Retired police officers always have sources; don't ask, and they won't tell. Pivotal to his reconstruction was his on-site investigation of the skid marks left by the patrol car, along with its front-end damage and the damage to the driver's side of Frank's truck. His analysis found that the patrol car was going east at about seventy-five miles per hour, not the fifty-five miles per hour the officer had stated in the report.

Also, the skid marks were straight, possibly indicating inattention at the time of the accident. Even a police officer responding to a call must travel at a safe rate of speed. In addition, the switch inside the patrol car that would activate the siren was in the off position. The switch for the exterior emergency lights was damaged and revealed nothing to shed light on its position at the time of the accident. Frank's truck had passed through two of the three lanes for eastbound traffic on this divided highway, indicating that the officer should have seen the truck before impact. He had indicated in the report that he didn't remember whether or not he saw it before impact.

During the discovery phase of the lawsuit, all the EMT (emergency medical technician) responders testified, as did Frank and the police officer, and each gave a different version of the accident. It was not until the trial that the drama began to unfold. One of the EMT personnel brought in a previously undisclosed portion of the ambulance report. As hard as I tried, I was not able to persuade the judge to keep the document from eventually being introduced into evidence. In this document was an entry referring to Frank that had the potential to cause us to lose the case. The entry was "a.o.b.," which the witness was prepared to testify was common parlance on Long Island for "alcohol on breath." I was able to keep that testimony and the document temporarily out of evidence and out of the hearing of the jury because it turned out that the witness on the stand was not the author of the entry. Until the author was produced, that portion of the document was hearsay and therefore excluded from evidence.

Of course, the next day, in came the EMT who was the author of that entry. Consequently, I was no longer able to keep the document from being introduced into evidence, although I still had the opportunity to cross-examine the author. My opening came when the witness was unable to recall smelling alcohol on Frank's breath or who else was present when the entry in the record was made. Fortunately, my prior experiences representing police officers in New York City enabled me to speak to several experienced accident responders during a lunch break that coincidentally took place during the cross-examination. I did this because it came out during the examination that this EMT, who was a volunteer, had in the past been an ambulance attendant in New York City. It was one of the best telephone calls I ever made. I discovered that, unlike on Long Island, the entry "a.o.b." in New York common parlance meant "aided on board."

"Aided" refers to the injured party, and "on board" refers to the call made to the hospital advising that the injured party is in the ambulance and on the way to the hospital. When confronted with this information, the EMT began crying uncontrollably from the witness stand, realizing that he was in error in not clearly indicating in the record what he meant by "a.o.b." and that his error had almost caused a gross miscarriage of justice.

Considering the circumstances, the judge was probably correct in denying my motion to strike any reference to alcohol from the record, leaving it to the jury to decide what "a.o.b." was meant to denote. To me, considering the amount of the settlement reached while the jury was out, the defendant wasn't going to take the chance of the jury awarding the plaintiff an excessive amount of money, and after talking to the jurors later, I confirmed that it was a good decision on the defendant's part. And so I say that while being cryptic may sometimes be witty, please, when in doubt, spell it out!

There but for the Grace of God Go I

Caution: You are about to enter a no-spin danger zone. There is nothing I can say or do that will make this a happy story. It is a story about courage and how a person can persevere under circumstances that most of us cannot fathom. It is a story that affected not only my client, Valerie, but also her family and anyone she came into contact with. There were also interesting issues of law that took place during my handling of her case that I hope will interest you, and I hope your life's experience will be enhanced by meeting her.

Valerie was like any happy-go-lucky, teenage schoolgirl living in your neighborhood. She was an above-average student, though a bit of an under-achiever, who loved sports and was adored by her family, consisting of her mother, father, and sister, Evelyn, who was a registered nurse. The accident occurred during the early-morning hours. The evening before, Valerie and her boyfriend, John, left her home for an evening out at about 7 P.M., with John driving Valerie's car. They headed east to attend a holiday party being given by John's employer, a company that owned a chain of several well-known fast-food stores. John was a managerial intern, and while attendance at the party was not mandatory, it was strongly suggested that all managerial employees attend, since speeches were to be given by management and awards distributed for work well done during the year. John was told that he was welcome to bring a date, in this case, Valerie.

They arrived at the catering hall at about 8 P.M. The food was excellent. There was wine at the table and a free open bar available throughout the evening. Everyone was left on their own to drink as much, or as little, as they chose. No one remembers anyone being drunk or unruly, keeping in mind that their employer, Big Brother, was watching over them.

The party ended at about midnight, at which time Valerie and John joined

167

several other couples in the coffee shop in the lower level of the building. To the best of everyone's recollection, no one drank any alcohol there. At about 1 A.M., Valerie and John left; again, John was driving. Wanting to do a little sightseeing, they decided to take a different parkway home and made a right turn while going west in order to enter the westbound lanes of that parkway. Unfortunately, they missed the entrance to the parkway, which they thought was on the left but actually was on their right. After traveling about a half-mile past the entranceway, mostly uphill, they realized their mistake and made a left turn onto a side street in order to safely make a U-turn and then make a right turn to retrace their route. Sadly unbeknownst to them, this side road was a horseshoe, and had they never made the U-turn, they would have exited at the other end of the road and on the other side of the crest of the hill, and it is unlikely that the accident would have happened. As they approached that right turn, John stopped at the stop sign, looked left, and when he was certain no one coming, started to make his right turn. His view to the left was limited since the crest of the hill was only about sixty feet to the left of the intersection. Unseen by them was a car traveling south at a speed in excess of seventy miles an hour while approaching that crest. It came over the hill and, without the driver ever hitting the brake, collided with the left rear of Valerie's car. There were no witnesses to the accident. When the first motorist came along and saw the scene of the accident, he knocked on the door of the nearest house, and the police were called. All involved in the accident were found to be unconscious. John remained in a coma for two weeks and had no memory of the accident. The driver of the other car was unconscious for about ten days and also had no memory of the accident. Apart from some facial scarring, John suffered only a broken leg, from which he recovered. The other driver had multiple fractures of his legs but also made a decent recovery, although he walked with a limp, which was likely to be permanent. Valerie was probably fortunate to be unconscious for about a month and also had no memory of the accident, which left her a quadriplegic, confined to a bed and wheelchair for the rest of her life.

Where do you start? Sadly, it was not the first time I had handled the case of a quadriplegic. I can tell you that the first visit with your client is an experience that stays with you. There are no right words to say. There simply is no way to know how your client feels.

At our initial meeting, Valerie's parents were also present, as was her sister. From the first day I met them to the last day several years later, I never saw more pain and sorrow in someone's face than in her father's. Both her mom and dad were wrought with pain. Her mom kept it inside. Her dad was unable to do the same. Under state law, the no-fault insurance carrier covering Valerie's car was initially responsible for her medical bills. That coverage, the basic $50,000, was gone in the blink of an eye. When that coverage is exhausted, the injured person's health coverage takes over, to the extent of that coverage.

Since Valerie was still a teenager living with her parents, she was considered to be an additional insured under her father's medical policy, which was a benefit paid for by his employer of seventeen years. Her father was an accountant employed by a financial broker, and the policy was one of the best on the market. At first subtly but then in an increasingly overt manner, his employer made life miserable for Valerie's father, hoping that he would quit and relieve them from the yearly increases to their health insurance premium, brought about by the enormous sums of money the insurance carrier was paying to Valerie's medical and health providers—in excess of $600,000 annually. However, sixty- to eighty-hour workweeks could not cause Valerie's dad to budge from his job. In addition, Valerie's sister pitched in, and she took over one of the eight-hour nursing shifts so that Valerie could spend more time with someone dear to her. Evelyn's husband never said a word, understanding his wife's concern for her sister. It was a family devoted to providing Valerie with the warmth and love she so desperately required.

Realizing immediately that the insurance policies covering Valerie's car and the other car could never come close to providing compensation for her injuries, I hired the best accident reconstruction expert I could find, and through his efforts developed a defective highway design theory and commenced action not only against the two drivers but also against the town, county, and village where the accident occurred. Leaving nothing to chance, I also included as defendants John and John's employer, under the theory that he was in the course of his employment at the time of the accident. I built this theory based upon the fact that, with my assistance in securing him a knowledgeable workers' compensation attorney, John had brought a claim for workers' compensation. His employer's workers' compensation carrier fought like a cornered lion, asserting every known defense and then even making up some. Their defenses ran the gamut of arguments. They asserted that John was drunk; that he didn't have to come to the party; that their actions, such as going for coffee in the diner and taking an alternate road which was not the shortest way home, broke the course-of-employment link; and even that the couple had pulled into the side street to have sex, which broke the course-of employment-link. As expected, however, they sent a rookie to John's worker's compensation hearing who was no match for John's seasoned attorney. It was no contest. The hearing officer ruled in John's favor at the end of the hearing. Based upon his findings of fact, set forth in his written decision, I moved for what is known as summary judgment against John's employer, asking the court, as a matter of law, to declare the employer to be responsible for John's negligence because there was now a finding that the accident occurred in the course of John's employment. The legal terminology is *respondeat superior* — the employer is responsible for the acts of its employee. After a ruling in my favor, the employer appealed, and the appellate court ruled that it would be a question for the jury, a ruling I could live with since I didn't believe that a jury would ever find against Valerie.

The highway design case was actually a little less complicated. My expert found that traveling in the direction he was going, the crest in the roadway presented a condition known as a limited visibility condition to the other driver. The New York State highway code required that a "Limited Visibility" sign be posted no more than a required distance from the crest of the hill to provide a warning to a motorist traveling in that direction that there was an intersection beyond the crest that the motorist could not see. That sign, which in fact had been posted, stood well beyond the maximum distance provided in the code, which presented the possibility that by the time the motorist reached the crest of the hill, he would forget the existence of the sign and it would be too late for him to react to the presence of a car exiting the side road. In addition, there was a speed sign so near that sign that it posed a distraction to the motorist, again a violation of the code.

All things considered, there was no doubt in my mind, or in the minds of the many defendants, that Valerie's case was going to a jury, which helped forge a settlement, contributed to by all concerned. I must applaud the attorney who represented the county; without his professionalism and compassion, the settlement might never have happened. He was a brilliant defense attorney, and his kind words lauding me for taking on this most challenging case have always meant a lot to me. Yes, an argument could be made that I should have taken the case all the way to a jury, but there surely would have been years of multiple appeals, and there remained the serious question of how long Valerie would live and the toll that a trial would take upon her. You see, quadriplegics have a limited life expectancy, since so many health complications can arise, the greatest among them kidney disease.

The first thing that Valerie did with a portion of her share of the money was to buy a house so that she could move out of her parents' house. She put the house in the name of her sister. The house was big enough for her sister and brother-in-law to also live there, which they did because they did not own a house of their own. Whether this was the beginning of the alienation between Valerie and her parents is hard to say. Gradually, they began to dwell on the fact that they had never approved of her relationship with John, who they felt would never amount to anything. Sadly, not long after the lawsuit was over, John, who also sued in a companion lawsuit and collected a modest sum of money, disappeared from the state and was never heard from again.

Valerie, despite her disabilities, enrolled in a college program which she physically attended (there was no internet at the time) with the benefit of a wheelchair-accessible van that she bought, driven by a nurse or sometimes her sister. She only had limited use of three fingers of her right hand and could not drive the van. She earned an undergraduate degree in psychology and went on to earn her master's degree. This was all done with the intent of getting a job as a psychologist, specializing in victims of accidents causing disability such as she had sustained. The problem that arose was that Valerie would lose her Social Security Disability monthly payments if she was employed and earning more than a bare minimum of money. Consequently, she was only able to perform volunteer work, which was enough to provide her with the sense of self-worth and joy she received from helping others such as herself.

It was in the course of her volunteer work that she met a practical nurse named Howard, who befriended her. Two years after they met, they announced their intent to marry.

Howard was a Nigerian-born man who had come to this country under a work program that led him to become a practical nurse. After their marriage, he moved into her home and spent his full days caring for Valerie. Her sister and brother-in-law accepted him into the home, welcoming the care and companionship he provided. Valerie's parents saw him as an interloper who was after her money. They resented the fact that she would not follow their advice and went ahead and married Howard anyway. They did not attend the wedding, and they ceased any contact with Valerie. In an attempt to rectify this schism, Valerie, with whom I kept in contact over the years, called me and asked that I draw a new will for her. After leaving what I considered a modest amount of money to Howard, she left the balance of her estate to her sister. Howard was present at her will signing and encouraged her in carrying out this plan. Sadly, this did not have a positive effect on her relationship with her parents, and that relationship, if anything, only went further downhill. On the five or six occasions that Valerie had to be hospitalized for kidney stone removal, bladder infection, or other systemic maladies, her parents never visited her in the hospital. They may have been kept informed by Valerie's sister, but I was never privy to those conversations.

On a November day, about one year after the will was signed, I received a telephone call that Valerie had passed away. She had died in her sleep from a heart attack. There were about ten people, including myself, in attendance at the funeral, which took place on a dark, drizzly day. Her parents did not attend. At her sister's request, I probated her will and distributed the funds. There was sadness in Howard's eyes as we shook hands at the grave site. Not the degree of sadness I saw in Valerie's dad's eyes, which persisted until the last day I saw him, about six weeks before the funeral. I would be remiss not to mention that her father had continued working, never leaving the job, so that Valerie could continue receiving her medical benefits to the day she died. He died about six weeks after she did. Although the death certificate listed natural causes, there is no question in my mind that if allowed, the cause of death would have indicated that he died of a broken heart. Think not harshly of him and always remember that "there but for the grace of God go I." In their own way, each of the people surrounding this incredible woman has left a deep, lasting, and indelible impression upon me, and I hope, by sharing this story, upon you too.

Acknowledgments

This book could not have been written without the love, friendship, and trust of many people. First, of course, is my loving and beautiful wife, Yael, without whom I simply would no longer exist. Also, I will always be grateful to several attorneys who, during my career, trusted me to represent their clients. Included are Sylvester (the "Commish") Garamella, Judge Vincent Rao, Sam Schaeffer, Jerry Silberstein, David Dean, and Justice Anthony Falanga, along with my law partners, Steve Tannenbaum and Craig Olson. I also would be remiss in failing to mention my very special secretary, Debbie Wenke, whose 20 years of dedication and expertise helped frame my career. Then there are the attorneys who engaged my services to act as trial counsel on behalf of their clients. Among them are Jerry Flynn and his partner, Bernie Jeffrey. It was Bernie who, with his brilliance, helped and guided me in making this book one that will contribute to the public's interest in and respect for the rule of law. Also worthy of note is my daughter, Amanda, also an attorney, who reviewed this work, along with my editor, Teresa Castle, and made me proud to present this book to the public. Lastly, a special thanks to all of my clients, who trusted me to represent them in their time of need. You all have my eternal thanks.